They went from
Cumbria

About the Author

David Murray is a retired international management consultant, formerly a partner in a global firm then working independently. In the later part of his career he was active in the field of corporate ethics, and on a voluntary basis in anti-corruption advocacy including many years as Deputy Chairman of Transparency International (UK).

An evangelical Christian preacher for more than sixty years David grew up among Brethren in East Lancashire. In younger years he was active in literature evangelism, co-organiser of an annual conference on evangelism and a trustee of the Lancashire Gospel Tent. He has been an elder in four churches, three of them with backgrounds in the Christian Brethren movement, and has served as visiting preacher and Bible teacher in a broad spectrum of evangelical churches.

He has served on bodies associated with the Evangelical Alliance, both UK and European, was for more than a decade chairman of the "Faith in Business" initiative then associated with the evangelical Anglican college at Ridley Hall, Cambridge, and has taught biblical principles of conduct in business, professional and public life on several continents.

Almost fifty years ago he commenced gathering information on the history of the Christian Brethren movement in the North of England, and now in retirement hopes to be able to make much of this available in print.

They went from
Cumbria

Heralds of the Cross
around the globe
from churches of the
Christian Brethren Movement
in 19th & 20th century Cumbria

by David J. Murray, M.A.

The Gospel Hall,
Corporation Road, Workington
2022

*Go into all the world
and preach the gospel.*

(Mark 16:15)

In loving memory of

my late parents

John and Alice Murray

who both pointed me to Christ

and brought me up in the 1950s

surrounded by the literature

of the early Christian Brethren

missionary movement.

Contents

Foreword

This book is a small offshoot from my longstanding (>40 years) project on the history of the Christian Brethren movement in the North of England. That still incomplete and unpublished work focuses chiefly on the origins, development, and too often the demise, of the local churches. These pages, in contrast, highlight some of the remarkable characters who emerged from these churches to spread around the globe, taking the message of Christ. Today, through their work, the testimony of the Gospel is often more vibrant there than here.

Eric Fisk once wrote about missionary life that "there are missionaries who carry on, day by day, week by week, ordinary routine work in hospitals, schools and compounds, when there appears to be little or no result in the spiritual sense. These missionaries are the salt of the Christian witness overseas. They are like infantry in battle. … Most missionaries live very busy lives; some few live interesting lives; a small minority live lives charged with change and excitement."

I have not deliberately selected the people about whom I've written in the book due to their fitting within any of these categories. There are, however, examples of them all. There is no "standard" missionary, and no one single model for the work. God calls individual people and gives them tasks to suit their individual abilities and personalities. We should also remember that foreign mission workers are fallible human beings just like ourselves, but I have made very few evaluative comments on them or their work. They report to their Lord in heaven. I am convinced that if they were today asked to review their own work they would point away from themselves and say, "See what God has done!"

Chapter lengths vary. There has been little attempt to standardise in this respect. To some extent this is due to the different numbers of years over which I have been collecting data on the individuals concerned. I have attempted as far as possible to discover what kind of people they were before their missionary lives and this has varied in its difficulty.

These are only examples of the many who went, not counting the cost, to serve in places far from home. Several others apart from the main subjects are referred to in the text.

Finally, I trust that what is produced here will both interest and inform, and should it stimulate others to go out into the world with the unchanging message of Christ Jesus, the Son of God crucified and risen for our salvation, in ways relevant to our contemporary world, I shall feel doubly rewarded.

Workington, October 2022.

Acknowledgements

The present book is not an academic-style work with detailed references and footnotes. At the same time I believe that credit should be given to the many sources of data and the individuals who have helped in making it all possible.

Firstly I must honour the work of the editors of *The Missionary Echo* (1872-1885) and *Echoes of Service* (from 1885 onwards) for their production of magazines from month to month that not only supplied fuel for prayer at the time but provided an immense historical resource to future generations.

Others, including those who have given help with individual chapters either during the writing or in past years of research, are listed in an appendix.

I also must record my special gratitude to my dear friend Mrs. Margaret James who read through the first draft of each chapter, and sometimes a second. Without her sharp eye this would have been a far poorer production. Needless to say any errors of fact or style that remain, probably added later, should all be credited to my own considerable fallibility.

Finally I must thank the assembly at Corporation Road Gospel Hall, Workington for allowing me space for office, library and archive in the rear hall, so freeing room in my small apartment to relax, less surrounded by boxes, bookcases and cabinets.

Introduction

There may be readers who wonder who are these Christian Brethren, and what was it that their missionaries went out to preach?

The Christian Brethren movement of the 19th century stood within the fold of historic Trinitarian Christianity, and still stands firmly there today. One God in three co-equal persons, Father, Son and Holy Spirit; the Son of God, sent by the Father, incarnate in this world as Jesus Christ, truly man and truly God, who died for our sins and on the third day rose again, ascended into heaven and one day will come again; the Holy Spirit present in this world, pointing sinners to faith in Christ, indwelling believers to empower them for service.

It is on the basis of this biblical evangelical Christianity that many men and women have gone, and still go, to the far corners of the earth in obedience to the command of the Lord Jesus, "Go into all the world and preach the gospel." Their service takes many forms. They may also be in healthcare, literacy and education, Bible translation work, and other forms of service, but underlying everything is the compulsion to preach, like the apostle Paul, "Christ died for our sins according to the Scriptures," and

"Believe on the Lord Jesus Christ and you will be saved."

As for church practice the Brethren movement sought for simplicity, abandoning hierarchies and organisation, seeing each local congregation as a free-standing church (assembly) accountable to the Lord alone and led by a plurality of elders rather than by a single head. They pray together, study the Scriptures together, evangelise together, each member contributing God-given abilities for the wellbeing of the whole. Missionaries did not seek to plant missionary-led churches but rather to teach and train the converts so that they became indigenous free-standing local churches. Idealistic? Certainly. Always fully achieved? No. But always the aspiration.

And in the background, a magazine launched in 1872 with one of its two office addresses in Kendal, here in Cumbria, *The Missionary Echo*, later renamed *Echoes of Service*. It developed further as a support organisation, but never as an employer of the missionaries; they always have and still do report solely to their Master in heaven, trusting him to supply their needs. This is "faith mission" in the mould of Anthony Norris Groves, father of Henry the *Echoes* founder, who first went out in the 1820s simply trusting God to provide.

Elizabeth Wilson

(Kendal and Shap to Inland China)

Elizabeth Wilson was born in 1828. She was a daughter of William Wilson, a prosperous Kendal manufacturer. He was one of the many evangelical Quakers who in the 1830s left the Quaker fold to join with the newly emerging Brethren assembly in Kendal. Later in the century one of her brothers, Robert Wilson, was a co-founder of the Keswick Convention.

Much of the distinctively Quaker 16th century style of speech acquired from her family in early years remained with Elizabeth to the end of her days and was still found in the phraseology of her letters into the early years of the 20th century.

From its very beginnings the Brethren movement had been evangelistically outward looking, not only in the British Isles but also overseas. This was strongly characteristic of the Kendal Brethren and there would be many opportunities for the young Elizabeth to learn of the spread of the Gospel around the world.

Her father had a cousin in London, Miss Mary Stacey, who was a member of the Tottenham assembly. During a holiday there as a young woman Elizabeth met a struggling young medical student from Barnsley in whom her cousin had taken an interest. Miss Stacey would pay his fares, make sure that he was given good meals, and had space to relax in her garden after the Breaking of Bread at Tottenham on Sundays. His name would become well-known in future years, J. Hudson Taylor, founder of the China Inland Mission.

Maybe Elizabeth was already drawn to China, or maybe it was conversation with Hudson Taylor that triggered the thought, but certainly from that time onward she knew that God was calling her to China to spread the gospel.

The young Elizabeth did not reach China. For thirty years she kept this longing substantially under wraps. Her mother needed her at home and she believed that responsibility to her parent must take priority for the present time. It was not that she was needed in the same way as in many families, to do the washing and cooking. The Wilsons had staff for those domestic activities. It was rather a matter of keeping a daughterly presence near at hand. For a number of years, in fact, Elizabeth did not live at the family home in Kendal but high up on the fells at Shap.

During her Shap years in the 1860s she was able to provide a meeting place for the little

Brethren assembly formed in the village. But why Shap? Was she quietly preparing herself for living away from the comforts of home in readiness for an eventual ministry in China? Did she spend many days out on the wild fells, walking the rough Westmorland landscape? If so, it would prove good preparation for the walking she was to do in later years on the other side of the globe.

After her mother's death it was only a matter of weeks before Elizabeth applied to the China Inland Mission. There was some hesitancy. Would a woman now approaching her fifties be able to cope with the rigours of Chinese travel? Would she be able to learn the language sufficiently well to be effective as a communicator of the gospel?

Hudson Taylor, however, was one of the very few who had known of her sense of call from those long years before. Having an independent income she was able to go without any dependence on CIM's very limited funds. So along with two other new recruits she set sail for China in early January 1876, arriving in Shanghai in mid-March.

Her work would be reported at various times both in the CIM's *China's Millions* and in the Brethren's *Missionary Echo*.

Initially Elizabeth spent months learning the Chinese language but was not good in health. She suffered in the intense heat and at one point considered taking a sea journey to Japan as the ocean air seemed to suit her and might help her to recover. This trip didn't happen but she regained her strength, and before long was ready for travel.

Hudson Taylor by this stage had leadership responsibility for dozens of missionaries, many of them still young and inexperienced. He had been back in England but toward the end of the year he returned and accompanied Miss Wilson (as she was then universally known, and as we'll now call her) on her first long journey to join up with a Mr. & Mrs. Bailer and their family who were going to settle in Nankin. It was there that she got her first taste of real missionary life. Dressed in Chinese native style she would walk out into the neighbourhood and along the river bank talking with the women, sharing the basics of the story of Jesus.

Chinese society at that time was very rigid, and not least as to the position of women. If women were to be reached with the gospel then women missionaries, and later female Chinese evangelists, were essential. Miss Wilson would visit their homes, accompanied by a Chinese lady who could help with interpretation where necessary, which at this stage was most of the time. Sometimes they would also take a male Chinese attendant as a safety precaution. Foreigners were the subject of deep suspicion in China at that time, especially the British because of their involvement in the great evils surrounding the opium trade. The danger was not insignificant, but Miss Wilson had an advantage, her age! Advancing years and white hair were revered, and this ensured her a better hearing and a greater measure of safety than might otherwise have been the case.

By mid-1877 she was on her travels again, and by 1878 she was at Wu-Chang near Hankow in Hu-peh Province with Mr. & Mrs. Charles Judd.

Arriving in Hu-peh province she was approaching an area of China that had been suffering from extreme drought. Starvation in some places halved the population around this time, and it was followed by cholera. The missionaries were not immune. Several died, and along with Mr. Judd she spent many weeks nursing another missionary in Hankow.

Still her travels were not over. In 1879 she embarked on a long journey into the interior with no male missionary as protection. There were just herself and a young lady recruit fresh to the country plus two Chinese servants. The following year, back in Kendal, a Methodist missionary whom she had met told his audience that as he left her "she was just starting upon a long and perilous journey, but he trusted that she would be greatly blessed in her efforts to do good among the people, and that her health and life would be preserved." This willingness to take what were considered to be major risks astonished many of the more conservative risk-averse, even much younger, missionaries. But she and her companion Miss Fausett trusted in God and went forward for over a thousand miles over many months to reach Han-chung.

It was there that for the next four years Miss Wilson evangelised locally, ran a basic dispensary to help with minor ailments, sometimes venturing further out into the surrounding countryside, and an occasional longer exploration into distant areas. Wherever she went she talked to the women about Jesus, and to the men when they would listen.

During these years she saw people come to faith in Christ, and even ten years later while visiting remote places other missionaries would come across people who already new of the life, death and resurrection of Jesus from when Miss Wilson and Miss Fausett passed through on their travels.

She and other missionaries had aspirations to take the gospel into areas that had resisted the presence of foreigners, such as the province of Hu-nan, but by 1885 she seriously needed a break. Her health was suffering. She was feeling the fact that she was advancing steadily toward sixty years old, so took a break down at the coast, at Shanghai. It was a long journey but much easier on boats going down the rivers than travelling an inland direction.

By March the following year Miss Wilson was on her way back, along with a few others, on the long journey to serve in Hu-nan. As they were still not permitted to live in that province they had to find accommodation at a place called Sha-shi, close to the border.

Her health, however, continued to be a problem. She got out and about as best she could but her activities were significantly restricted by lack of energy. Her letters at this time suggest that she realised that her years of service may be coming to a close, but still she wrote in February 1887, "I go as I can and when I can. ... I have no doubt that the Lord will give me just the right work as I wait on Him and He gives me strength."

Eventually she had to face the reality. She had been in China without a furlough for twelve years. She needed to go home for a long rest.

Her nephew Dr. William Wilson had for some years been running a hospital at Han-chung and was returning home on furlough. She accompanied him and his wife, arriving back in England just before the end of 1887.

Hudson Taylor wrote of her that it was not at all certain that her health would recover to the point of allowing a return to China, "but I do know that her life there has been an immense blessing."

Possibly the best summary of her life and ministry comes from the CIM annual report in 1883 when, of course, she still had several more years service ahead of her. In looking forward to settling in Sha-shi a letter referred to Miss Wilson's expected acceptability to the people of that often hostile area. The editor added an explanatory footnote as follows.

"Miss Wilson's age gives her weight with the Chinese, and her influence is greatly increased by her loving, joyful spirit, which spreads cheerfulness and inspires confidence among all around her. ....."

"Her mature Christian experience has been greatly valued by both missionaries and converts. In many ways she has rendered valuable help, and has not feared to undertake journeys to remote provinces. The Lord, whom she has trusted, has not failed her, and her noble example may have a voice to others."

Elizabeth returned to her extended family in Kendal, sometimes staying at Shap as in younger years, sometimes in rest homes provided for retired missionaries. She did not herself return to China but had the comfort that her nephew Dr. William Wilson had been out there serving as a missionary doctor since 1882, and other members of her extended family and friends were joining the work.

Elizabeth Wilson lived on into the 20th century, dying in 1916 at the age of 88.

George Spooner

(Shap to Spain and Argentina)

In our opening chapter we saw Elizabeth Wilson, of Kendal and Shap, leaving for China in early 1876. Later in the same year the little village of Shap saw another of its people leave for missionary service overseas. George Spooner left for Spain.

Spain was one of the countries that attracted a great deal of missionary attention in the growing Brethren movement during the second half of the nineteenth century. To a great extent this was due to the interest and encouragement of two outstanding Christian leaders in the movement, Robert ("R.C.") Chapman of Barnstaple and George Muller of Bristol.

This was not an easy mission field. Religious liberty fluctuated according to the government in power. For years under Queen Isabella it had been a criminal offence to sell a Bible, and effectively even to own one. Only the Roman Catholic priests had that privilege. The majority taught little of it to their parishioners, and certainly had no wish to see copies freely distributed. There was little or no Protestant presence in most parts of the country and

Bible-based preaching calling people to repentance and a personal faith in Christ was totally unknown in most towns and cities.

Missionaries such as George Lawrence, who first went to the country in 1863 at a time when persecution was strong, came close on several occasions to being arrested. Once Lawrence and colleagues, after only just managing to escape over the border into France, were tried in their absence and sentenced to nine years penal servitude on a prison ship. This made it difficult to risk returning, until at last in 1868, and again in 1870, restrictive laws were overturned.

Among those who caught the vision of biblical gospel preaching in Spain were two young men in the north of England, Thomas Blamire and James Wigstone. In 1870, aged 22 and 20 respectively, they left Carlisle and Penrith to prepare themselves for the work, studying in London at the college of the great Baptist preacher, Charles Haddon Spurgeon. Two years later they went first to Madrid then to Galicia in the north of the country, to the cities of A Coruña and Vigo.

Although from Congregational church backgrounds and trained in a Baptist college they went out as independent missionaries unaffiliated to any denomination or missionary society, simply trusting the Lord to provide their support as was the practice among missionaries from Brethren assemblies, with which (in Carlisle and Penrith) they were by now associated. Their activities over many years were reported both in Baptist and Brethren publications.

George Spooner's Pre-Missionary Years

Born in 1845, George Spooner came to faith in Christ at the age of 19 and shortly afterwards became interested in overseas mission. Living at Shap he came into contact with Blamire and Wigstone, although he himself at first was interested in missionary outreach to China. Was this possibly the influence of Miss Wilson?

There were problems in China at the time and to go there was not feasible so George devoted himself to evangelistic work, largely in the North of England.

In the early 70s he would be kept up to date with the work of the two Cumbrians in Spain by the newly launched magazine, *The Missionary Echo.* Mr Henry Groves, one of its two founder-editors, lived in Kendal and encouraged George in his aspirations for overseas service. Another source of advice, at a distance, was R. C. Chapman, and it also seems likely that he would be in touch with at least Wigstone (who had lived nearby in Penrith) by post.

In June 1876 in the Brethren meeting room at Bowness (now the Gospel Hall and the recording studio for Radio Outreach) he conducted the wedding service for a young man living in Shap, whose bride was a Bowness girl. Then a few months later, at the age of 31, he was in Spain.

Familiarisation in Spain, 1876-78

Having been formally commended to his new work in Spain by the Shap assembly he went initially to Barcelona. *The Missionary Echo* reported on the departure of a large group led by veteran missionary George Lawrence. Some of the group were starting their first terms, while others were returning.

Among the returnees was James Wigstone. He had come back to Penrith briefly a couple of years earlier in order to marry Miss Mary Workman and then returned with her to Spain. Just over a year later she had died after giving birth to a daughter. Family back in Penrith were now caring for the child, until two years later he remarried. Thomas Blamire and his wife Rosetta were also in the party, he having returned for a break due to health problems.

George's first period in Spain lasted somewhat less than two years. Language learning was the first big challenge. He spent this time with the two younger men, Blamire and Wigstone, in the city of A Coruña and its surrounding area.

Although Blamire and Wigstone were younger than Spooner they by now had several years of Spanish experience behind them. They were very much in the lead and were able to go out into the surrounding areas while George was working at the language.

Eventually he was able to join with them more as they sold Bibles and preached the gospel to any who would listen. Gradually his language skills developed. As well as A Coruña itself they rented a house in Arteijo, a village eight miles away, and held meetings there at which some came to faith in Christ. They also started to plan for work in Ferrol which Blamire and Wigstone had visited in 1875.

England and Marriage, 1878

There was, however, something drawing him back to Westmorland. The Bowness assembly of the Christian Brethren was one of the oldest in the north of England, dating back to the 1830s. The Martin family played an important part in it for many years. The young Bowness lady at whose wedding George had officiated shortly before leaving for Spain had a cousin, 23-years-old Mary Ann Martin.

It was to this cousin that George himself, now 34, was married in August 1878, again at the Bowness meeting room. The service was conducted by another friend from Shap days, Thomas Boxall, who by this time was one of the key leaders in the young Penrith assembly.

Following their marriage the Spooners did not leave immediately for Spain, and during these months he demonstrated his willingness to adopt some of the latest technology to assist in communication of the gospel. "Dissolving views" were among the latest forms of "lantern slide" in which there was a gradual transition from one projected image to the next. To people today it may seem quite primitive, but this was before the days of moving pictures and these were very popular. According to a local press report, in the November at "the Brethren's Room" in Bowness he used his equipment for an "exhibition" on Joseph and his Brethren. He was using materials that he'd trialled while in Shap two years earlier.

Ferrol, 1878-81

They reached Spain in mid-December and settled not in A Coruña but in the industrial and port city of Ferrol ninety minutes away by ferry, where there was also a large military establishment.

A small evangelical group already existed there, the fruit of earlier visits by Messrs. Blamire and Wigstone and also by Baptists. A Swedish itinerant preacher Mr. Lund had been working together with an almost blind Spanish evangelist who had moved away and later died, while the newly married Mr. Lund had left for Valencia. He was happy for George to take responsibility for caring for the converts. When George and Mary arrived there were thirteen in the fellowship.

In early January George wrote, "I have commenced a day-school in my house for the present, as the dear children have been ejected from the government school because they attend the Sunday school, and their parents are Christians, or Protestants, so called." Where they were living was not very convenient so quickly they started to look for accommodation for home, school and meeting room in a more central area.

They lived here in Ferrol for three years. It was not plain sailing. Since the revolution of 1868 and the later accession of King Alfonso there had been relaxation of the rigid anti-Protestant laws of Queen Isabella's reign. However, priestly opposition at a local level was still intense. False accusations were laid against them and every attempt was made to deny them places to meet and to preach. The law was twisted against them, and at times the help of the British consul had to be called upon.

In the September of their first year they had joy from the birth of a daughter, but opposition from the priests intensified. Already the landlord of their meeting room had been pressurised to cancel their tenancy, but refused to do so. Now their school teacher and family were ejected from their home.

It could sometimes even be difficult to find food. People had been told by the priests that they should not sell to these Protestant preachers. An elderly Christian lady would sometimes travel by night to other towns and under cover of darkness bring back food for the Spooners.

But opposition does not kill the gospel. The message of salvation, forgiveness of sins, by faith in Christ alone, and not by religious effort or ceremony, was used by the Holy Spirit to bring some to turn to God from their idols. Then in 1881 a change of government brought another increase in freedom.

It was while they were at Ferrol that they had a visitor from Cumbria. The early accounts of the *Missionary Echo* show that among the Spooners' regular financial supporters was the assembly in Whitehaven (now at Sandhills Lane). One of the younger leaders there was 35-yr-old Daniel Combe who would continue as an elder well into the 20th century and was a man with a passion for overseas mission.

In 1881 Daniel Combe was a young widower with small children. His parents had his family while he sailed for a visit to Ferrol. His report, published in the *Missionary Echo*, gives a fascinating insight into the work there as seen by an outsider. He accompanied George and some of his colleagues to several places in the countryside around Ferrol. Sales of Gospels, Bibles and New Testaments were at this period going well, a marked change since the recent relaxation of the law.

Education was an important aspect of missionary service in Spain at that time. The veteran George Lawrence had started schools some years before and now there were several, many of them supported by George Muller. After all, it was well and good to sell Bibles but people needed to be able to read them and literacy was far from universal. As already mentioned a small school had been started in

Ferrol and the assembly in Kendal helped toward the salary of the teacher. By November of their first year the Spooners had managed to rent a home in which they could live upstairs while adapting the downstairs area, by removing partitions and whitewashing walls, to use as a meeting hall and schoolroom.

In mid-1881 they were joined by another missionary, George Chesterman. He had previously with his wife settled in Barcelona but the climate did not suit his wife's health. They had decided to move to the north although it was some time before she was able to come, having gone to recover in England.

Another visitor from England was the widely respected Mr. Henry Dyer who reported that the school in the hall under the Spooners' home had enrolled forty-five pupils, although some had been taken away and the priests had opened in competition next door.

A Coruña, 1881-84

Looking at the pattern of work in both Ferrol and A Coruña during 1881 the missionaries felt somewhat minded to move their base across the water to the larger city. A Coruña was more central to the region that they'd been reaching over the past five years. Blamire and Wigstone had both now gone to other areas and the church there was in need of greater help. It would also be easier to visit and support the little church in Arteijo. Keeping in touch with the Ferrol believers from A Coruña would not be difficult. The ferry times were more convenient for the return journey in that direction than for helping A Coruña from Ferrol. Unfortunately though, a new hall would have to be found to replace the one under their home.

The move did not happen straight away. It took time but in November 1881 George and Mary Spooner and their young children, along with George Chesterman, moved to A Coruña. Almost immediately the latter had to leave for England to join his wife as she recovered her health, and it would be January of 1883 before the two of them returned.

In A Coruña as in Ferrol there was continual opposition. Preaching in the open air was legal (provided there was no singing!) but attacks and insults were common. In spite of this many people listened and some came to the indoor meetings in the hall. The missionaries also had the support of Spanish believers who could share in the preaching.

People in the locality had learned to expect that when someone believed the gospel their lives would be changed. There would be no more drunkenness, stealing, wife-beating and adultery. If someone professed the faith but didn't change they would be mocked. The churches were being strengthened. Some older believers died. Funerals were often attended by large numbers who had seen the changed lives. Indeed at one the crowd was so great that there was surprise that no-one was injured in the crush. These times gave more opportunity to present the gospel and several believed as a result of what they heard at a funeral.

The two Georges regularly went out into the countryside, over the hills, through the forests, across the fields and by the sea. They walked, both to populated and out of the way places. They carried their bags of Bibles, Testaments and Gospels, speaking to people and selling the books whenever they could.

It could be dangerous work. On one occasion they came across a group of travelling musicians. These were armed with stout sticks primarily for their own defence, but they were also perfectly willing to use them aggressively against the preachers. A speedy departure was necessary and they escaped unharmed. Health was sometimes a problem but the outdoor exercise was helpful. Back at the churches attendance, both by believers and enquirers, was good. Progress was encouraging.

Betanzos, 1884-87

After two and a half years based in A Coruña the Spooners moved again, this time to Betanzos, a town further inland. Two years before, Gorge had written, "One of our brethren visited his native place near Betanzos, at carnival time, with Bibles, &c., and was much encouraged with the reception he got, and the earnestness with which the people listened. ... In four days he made fifty-six sales. I am anxious to open a [hall] in Betanzos shortly if the Lord will."

Now in 1884 he writes that they had been praying for some years for an opportunity to open up work in this town. By August a hall was ready for use, converted from an old wine store. George and Elizabeth Chesterman stayed in A Coruña, and were there for almost thirty years.

There was opposition here as elsewhere. Mary Spooner wrote shortly after their arrival in Betanzos that the priest never failed to use an opportunity to tell the people "that we are sons of the Devil". Another priest was collecting Bibles and publicly burning them. Young men throwing stones frightened people away and for a time it was necessary to have two policemen standing nearby during services to stop serious attacks. Having said that, by early the following year they were having encouraging times with young people studying the Bible.

Despite all the challenges there were opportunities. A visitor, commenting on the frequency of fairs at Betanzos wrote, "On these occasions Mr. Spooner has a small stall in the open market-place for selling Bibles and portions of Scripture. I noticed that there was a much greater crowd around him than around any other stall in the fair. He commences early in the morning and continues throughout the heat of the day, until three or four in the afternoon, telling out the gospel and answering questions."

There were encouragements as people read the Scriptures they'd bought. One young man who had been a strong opponent started to read the Bible with the interested young people. Two young men were baptised. Also it was around this time that one of Mary's sisters came to join them.

Then in September of 1886 George wrote about a number of Spanish believers who had escaped the stresses of persecution by emigrating to South America.

There was no indication in this letter that after spending almost twelve years, including nine as a married couple, the Spooners' own time in Spain was coming to an end. He had been considering a trip back to England for a break, but family circumstances brought this forward and in early 1887 George and Mary moved back to Bowness with their six children before leaving once again, not back to Spain but to a new sphere of service in another Spanish-speaking country on another continent.

Argentina, 1887-94

After a short time at Bowness, at the age of 41, George left for Argentina. Mary remained in Bowness where her brother William had a grocery business. Sadly while George was away their youngest child died but in late 1889 Mary Ann, now 34, took the remaining family across the Atlantic to join him in Santa Fe province.

George had been working for the railway company by day, and evangelising by night. Now, after the family's arrival, he was invited to take charge of a Sailors' Home in the port city of Rosario, two hundred miles upstream from Buenos Aires on the Paraná River .

Their home there became a magnet for Christian sailors arriving in the port, and also for many who were seeking the Saviour. A small church was established, for several years meeting in the home until eventually a meeting hall was opened.

George did not confine himself to Rosario. Just as in Spain he would ride out into the surrounding areas, taking a stock of Bibles. Often in fellowship with other missionaries and national preachers, meetings would be held and George would both preach the gospel and teach the new believers.

Then came cholera. At 48 years old George Spooner went to meet his Saviour.

He had recently been away in Cordoba for two weeks visiting another missionary, Will Payne, helping with some baptisms. He preached nightly during the second week, stressing the eternal security of the one who believes in Jesus. More came to faith in Christ, others to a greater sense of assurance; several were baptised and the Cordoba fellowship was growing. Mr. Payne said they would have loved to keep him there but realised he must return to Rosario. George himself was having thoughts of possibly moving to Cordoba to help build up the developing work.

But it was not to be. Just over three weeks later Will Payne received an urgent message from Mary Spooner. Her husband was ill. He set off immediately but arrived too late. George was already buried, and the following day they also buried nine-year-old Gershom who had died from the same disease as his father.

So far as I am able to tell from the materials available to me Mary Spooner's chief role during the years in Spain seems to have been with her family and using her home for what now we might call hospitality evangelism.

Over nine years she had borne six children. Now in her late thirties she was to have sole responsibility for the surviving five, all under ten years old, no small task. She stayed in Argentina caring for the family and earning an income, but also she developed her own service for the Lord. Along with Mrs. Leonard George she carried on with the ministry to seamen and others in the port area. Many were blessed.

Several of the children and grandchildren preached the same life-transforming message as their parents for decades to come, some as full-time missionaries.

Back in Spain the work around A Coruña continued, George Chesterman worked with courage and energy in taking the Word of God out into the surrounding areas, frequently on his bicycle, until in 1910 after almost three decades they returned to England due to recurring health problems.

In that area of Galicia today there are several assemblies, some of them flourishing. The work in Betanzos did not prosper. The persecution was so severe. As already mentioned, the work in A Coruña continued, and the Ferrol church revived in the early 20th century. The assembly in A Coruña is today the oldest Protestant church in Galicia. George Spooner also shared in work at the beginning of the assemblies in Marin and Seixo, and they became the largest Protestant churches in the Northwest. Marin is still thriving. The legacy of the Spooners remains into the 21st century.

James Wharton

(Barrow to North America)

The 1870s saw major development in the Christian Brethren movement all around what is now Cumbria. During the decade new assemblies were either first formed or saw a surge in growth in Carlisle, Penrith, Workington, Kirkby Stephen and more. Another important focal point was the new town of Barrow-in-Furness, growing from a small hamlet to a major centre with its steel and shipbuilding industries over a very few years. People arrived from many parts of the country, and among them was a man in his early twenties, originally from Penrith, James Wharton by name.

He was closely associated with other men such as Thomas Robinson, William (always "W. B.") Hargreaves and Christopher Johnson (later in Cockermouth). They were respected elders in later years but at that time energetic and enthusiastic young men. They joined together in evangelism, pointing people to Jesus Christ as the only Saviour. Many different approaches were used, one being the conduct of Open Air Meetings at a popular place in the centre of the town known as The Fountain. James Wharton was one of those preachers who could hold a crowd as he spoke of sin, divine judgement, repentance and faith. Many came to faith in Christ. At a later date in the1890s the present writer's grandfather was challenged by the gospel for the first time in his life while passing preachers at the Fountain on his way to a football match.

Along with their evangelistic outreach they were also keen to establish a church on simple New Testament lines without the rituals or structures of the traditional denominations, and meeting only to the name of the Lord Jesus Christ with no other distinguishing label. From this came eventually the Abbey Road Gospel Hall. This was James Wharton's church background?

But who was he? What were his origins? In his early years no-one would have expected him to become a preacher and church leader of any kind, let alone one active not only across the North of England but even across the Atlantic. He grew up in an irreligious family environment, his father being the landlord of the "Golden Keg" pub in Penrith. He and his younger brother John did, however, get some Christian input from a Sunday School, then often known as "Sabbath School". They were allowed to attend the one at the local

Congregational church but it meant little to him. As a young teenager he started an apprenticeship with a shopkeeper in town but left and went off to join a ship and see the world.

After five years at sea, living the life of a rough godless sailor, he returned to Penrith. The prodigal may have returned, but there was no father to welcome him as in the biblical story. His parents had both died while he was away. He went back to the shopkeeper whom he had left, and amazingly was accepted back to complete his apprenticeship. It was during this period somewhere around 1870 that, sitting in the living room of an elderly lady (I like to think, though without any evidence, that it may have been his old Sunday School teacher who had prayed for him down the years) he responded in faith to the Christ who had died to bring him forgiveness, and committed his life to the Lord's service.

He married, and with his new wife Sarah moved to Barrow. How he got started in business I don't know but being an energetic young man with Sarah's help he built up a business as a furniture dealer, eventually with a shop on Forshaw Street in the town centre.

As we've seen already he was involved in evangelism in Barrow. He also became known as a gospel preacher in nearby areas on the Furness Peninsula, but he was now to have his horizons widened even further. Had he visited the Southern States of the USA during his years away at sea? We don't know, but another influence could well have been an article printed in the recently launched magazine *"The Missionary Echo"* appealing on behalf of the spiritually neglected communities of freed slaves. Slavery had been abolished throughout the British Empire in 1837 and in the United States of America in 1865, but the treatment of the freed men and women in the Southern States could only be described as appalling. Most lived in primitive conditions, strict separation of the races was insisted upon, and the gospel of Jesus Christ which transforms people's lives was little understood.

Whatever the influences on him, James Wharton himself later wrote a piece for the *Echo* in October 1876. At 27 years old he wrote it having just arrived in New Orleans, having gone there at his own expense for six months. Sarah was back at home in Barrow looking after the business while he was surveying the ground to assess the need and see what he could possibly do. For the next twenty five years James spent large parts of each winter in America, and after the first two or three years Sarah often went with him, developing her own parallel ministry to women combining practical teaching of domestic skills with spiritual input, evangelism and Bible teaching.

On that first visit in 1877 he knew not a single person in the city of 200,000 people, so how to start? He prayed, went to see the chief of police, got permission to preach in the open air, got up on a bale of cotton in a prominent place, sang a hymn or two, and began to preach of God's love to all. A few people gathered round and listened so he went back at the same time each day. The numbers grew, the first few people came to faith in Christ, and so he continued. He also visited from house to house and saw more conversions from this work. Commenting on the spiritual environment he said that he had looked at what the existing churches were doing but it was all inside their walls, not going out to the people.

He came across a very rare worker among the coloured population, a lady from the Northern States who worked among children and young people, running classes and fellowship groups to encourage and teach not only the gospel but basic standards of Christian living. The people themselves were praying for others to come and help them but few took up the challenge.

It was not until October 1880 that he was able to go for a second visit, and this time he was accompanied by a younger colleague, Richard Irving. They preached sometimes together and sometimes in different places. More came to Christ, they began to gather with a few of the new believers to break bread in memory of the Lord, bread reminding them of his body broken as he died for our sins, and wine the outpouring of his life blood for our salvation.

This time he also commenced something that was to be of great strategic significance in the future. He began work among students. In future years he was able to speak of students who through this early ministry had responded to Christ's call to trust and serve him and were now in teaching and other professional fields right across the Southern States, involved in the educational and spiritual formation of the next generation. The gospel was having not only an inner spiritual effect but an external moral and practical impact for good in people's lives and homes.

As already mentioned, Sarah went with him on many occasions after the first two exploratory visits, balancing this somehow with bringing up their young family (two boys and a girl), the boys attending school in America during at least some of their time there. But Sarah did not restrict her self to domestic duties. She ran classes for young coloured women in subjects such as hygiene and the care of the sick. She taught Bible classes, and her addresses and study materials were complimented in the press. She gave time to the Railroad Men's Mission organising the distribution of food and clothing to the most needy, visiting the poor and sick in their homes. Sarah Wharton was not only a missionary's wife but a missionary in her own right. The fruits were long-lasting, and some of her young women Bible class students became missionaries in other lands.

After years of his annual winter visits James several times wrote that conditions for those who had been freed from slavery were in many ways not getting better. Segregation laws were strict. This also impacted on his own work and that of the few people who were seeking to do something similar. They could preach to white people and that was acceptable, but to minister among the black population meant exclusion from white circles. The work was attacked in the press, including challenges to the legality of what they were doing. The idea of whites being so closely involved with coloured people was offensive to the segregationist majority of Southern whites, even to those who claimed to be followers of the Christ who treats all races as equal before God. His own philosophy was to treat everyone, black and white, with equal respect and to assume him to be an upright citizen "until such time as he proved to be a rogue".

Eventually James gave up his business back in England. He still spent half the year in England and half in America. In the summer months for many years he worked a Bible Carriage around country areas of England. This meant, of course, that he was no longer self-financing and in common with many other missionaries he simple trusted God to provide, which He did through the kindness and generosity of his people who wanted to have fellowship with the work. One of his colleagues in that work later went to the States, set himself up as a fruit farmer and preached the gospel in his spare time in a majority coloured area, no doubt a fruit of conversation with James.

During his American visits James was constantly worried by the lack of Biblical knowledge among church leaders in the coloured communities, and too often also among the whites. He did his best to encourage serious Bible study. As to questions of church order he taught the converts to meet in Biblical simplicity as he himself had learned to do years before in Barrow, to pray and study the Scriptures together and to break bread weekly in memory of the Lord. This did not mean, though, that he isolated himself from those who followed different patterns of church life. Indeed in 1895 he was preaching evangelistically to large congregations in a city centre Congregational church and the magazine *The Coloured American* could report that he had "preached and conducted revival services" in almost all the largest colleges, universities and institutions of almost all denominations in the South. Where the Gospel of the transforming power of Christ was able to be preached James Wharton would go there and preach it.

From 1891 onwards his work was no longer reported in Echoes of Service but he continued through the 90s and into the new century, making the two-way voyage across the Atlantic well over twenty times. A newspaper advertisement for a Penrith evangelistic campaign in 1902 says, "Mr. Wharton, who is a native of Penrith, ... laboured among the freed slaves of America for over 25 years and during that time has seen hundreds turn to the Lord."

From the 1890s onwards, with the Abbey Road assembly in Barrow still as his home base, James Wharton was frequently seen working among the Brethren assemblies of Cumbria. He had not forgotten his native land. Workington in 1892, Frizington in 1893, Bowness in 1895, his native Penrith repeatedly (1903, 1904 and 1907 for example) were only some of the places where he conducted evangelistic campaigns. However, the years were passing, and eventually he could no longer sustain the American work. With the help of God he had made a positive difference to the lives of many, but it was time to slow down.

He left less by way of official public record than the many people. The census returns every ten years had a habit of missing him; during those months he was in America. However, in the 1921 census he at last appears along with Sarah at 89 Abbey Road, Barrow-in-Furness, both listed as "Retired Furniture Dealers". From the public record no-one would know of the extensive international ministry of this man of God. He died aged 79 at his Abbey Road home on 25th February 1928.

He was survived by Sarah, who was by now 83 years old. More than thirty years earlier the *Coloured American* magazine had reflected on her part in the ministry using the language of the Old Testament book of Proverbs. Many "shall arise up and call her blessed".

Mary, Edith & Mabel Brown

(Whitehaven to India and China)

Affixed to a building wall on Queen Street, Whitehaven is a plaque in honour of Dame Edith Brown, or to give her full honours,

> "Edith Mary Brown, DBE, Kaisar-I-Hind (Gold 1922), MA (Cantab), MD (Brux), FRCSEd, MRCOG."

The plaque, placed there by the Whitehaven & District Civic Society in 1996, goes on to describe her work as a medical missionary and educator. Clearly this was an exceptional woman.

My inclusion of the Brown family might be challenged as although it is true that they went to India and China they did not go from Cumbria but from elsewhere in the country.

They were, however, certainly missionaries with Christian Brethren associations and were born in Whitehaven, three from a family of six children with widespread missionary interests and involvements.

The Brown Family

Edith Brown (1854-1956) was the fifth of six children of George Wightman Brown, who for around twenty years from the mid-1840s was the manager of the Bank of Whitehaven. At the time of her birth the building at No. 9 Queen Street was the office of the bank, the substantial apartment above it being accommodation for the manager and his family. George Brown, however, was not only a prominent citizen of the town with a key role in its economy. He was also the founder, humanly speaking, of the assembly of Christian Brethren which today meets (as it has for over a century) in the former Friends' Meeting House on Sandhills Lane.

George was married twice, his first wife Caroline Culverwell (1818-1853) was born in Exeter and, although she was living with her parents in Manchester when she met the young banker and married him, her Devon connections would prove important in the lives of the next generation. There were three children from this first marriage, a son and two daughters. One of these older daughters, Mary Louisa (born 1846) was later, as we'll see, to spend the early years of her married life in India. The Devon and India missionary connections of the Brown family were extensive.

Sadly Caroline Brown died in 1853. George did not remarry quickly but in 1861 Mary Walther of London became his second wife and there were three daughters from this second marriage, Lucy Theodora (1862), Edith Mary (1864) and Mabel Walther (1867). None of the three ever married, but two of them became missionaries, Edith to India and Mabel to China.

In 1871 George Brown was tragically killed in an accident involving a startled horse while on the way to collect his two elder daughters from the Braithwaite station for a holiday at the cottage he owned high on the Whinlatter road above Braithwaite. At the time of their father's death Caroline and Mary Louise were in their mid-twenties and still living at home in Whitehaven. Their brother John was twenty-eight, married, living in Manchester. Of the younger children Mabel was only four years old, Edith not yet seven and Lucy nine when they lost their father.

Their mother now moved with the whole family to Manchester. After two years there Caroline in 1873 married Walter Ashby, a miller and (vegetable) oil merchant with his business in Reigate, Surrey. A few years later Mrs. Brown moved to Croydon, less than ten miles from Reigate, with the younger children who were by now in their teens.

Lucy appears to have lived with her mother right up to the latter's death, not having any occupation outside the home. Mabel also lived with her mother and sister, but worked first as a governess and later as a teacher and then examiner at the Civil Service Department of King's College, London. Mabel will be the eventual subject of this chapter but first we must look, albeit rather briefly, at Mary, the middle daughter from George Brown's first marriage, and Edith, the middle daughter from his second.

Mary Louise (Brown) Bowden

Back in 1836 William Bowden was one of two young men who, with their recently married wives, went from Barnstaple in Devon to the Godavari Delta on the eastern side of India. They were the first recruits of Anthony Norris Groves the Brethren missionary pioneer following his initial exploration into India after leaving Baghdad. (See mention of Groves in the Introduction and also page 67.)

Because of his Cumbria connection we should note that when they had been in India for some years they were joined by a Westmorland man whose life story fully merits more attention but which we have to pass over quickly. Thomas Heelis was born at the Rectory in Appleby but went to sea as a young man with few thoughts of God. It was noticing the manner of life of a poor low caste Indian sweeper on his ship, and discovering from him that it was Christ who had changed his life, that started Thomas on his road to faith and ultimately his call to a long life of missionary service.

Moving on a couple of decades from there, in 1858 during his first furlough back in England William Bowden came to Whitehaven and spoke at a conference on overseas mission, surely the result of the Brown family's Devon connections. Their interest in India is also shown by a surviving note which records how pleased they were during their Braithwaite holidays to see the interest in India shown by the assembly at Keswick.

One of the six sons of William Bowden, Edwin, followed his father into full-time missionary service working from a house boat in which he moved up and down the rivers and canals of the Delta. Another son, Frederick Henry, went into the insurance business, eventually setting up his own firm, but did not forget the reason why his family was in India. He was an enthusiastic evangelist and spent substantial amounts of his time, and money, reaching out himself with the gospel and helping others who had little financial support. He was never listed as a missionary in the full-time sense, but he and his young wife were most certainly involved in active mission, and in a far more than casual manner. That wife was Mary Louise Brown.

They were married in 1873 at Manchester, Frederick being 29 and Mary 27. Shortly afterwards they were on their way to India. The ship stopped at an Italian port, and as they were walking around the city streets they spotted a Bible Society shop. Grabbing the opportunity they went in, bought a stock of New Testaments and gospels and distributed them among the crowds. Once in India they quickly became involved in evangelistic outreach alongside Fred's business interests.

Not themselves being listed as missionaries out on "faith lines" meant that their work was not directly reported in *The Missionary Echo* but from time to time they are mentioned by other workers. In March 1878, for example, a letter from Narsapur: "Dear Mr. and Mrs. Fred Bowden are here just now. They have recently been holding a fortnight's meetings at a village about six miles from this. The Lord has blessed the Word, and several have professed faith in Jesus."

Fred and Mary had four children, three of whom were born in India. Alongside bringing up her family and involvement in evangelistic work she was also known as one who cared deeply for the wellbeing of the missionaries working in the often harsh Indian climate. In 1881: "Mrs. F. Bowden has just returned from nursing Miss Reade. She heard of her illness a fortnight ago, and set off at once, and stayed at Punrooty till she and her husband brought Miss Reade in to Madras, and left her there with kind friends, where she will have every attention. ... Her energy and forgetfulness of self [is] manifestly God-given, so that the heathen are amazed at her."

Also the business enabled financial support to be provided in cases of need. In 1884, for example, when his father's old colleague John Beer needed to return ill to Britain but could not afford it, "The Lord in great grace provided the passage-money for him and his family through Br. F. Bowden, so that no sooner was the need clearly manifested than the supply was ready."

Leaving his insurance business to some of his brothers, Henry had set up as a manufacturer of patent Indian medicines, firstly in Madras and then, after in the mid-1880s in England. Both he and his eldest brother William were involved in the production and marketing of the widely popular soothing ointment Bowden's Balm, based on a formula written in Sanskrit and given to their father years before as a mark of gratitude by an elderly fakir. Bowden's Balm is still today commemorated in Devon, at the Barnstaple museum. For many years that ancient Indian medicine helped support the work of missionary outreach. Fred lived until 1922 and was survived by Mary who is said to have emigrated to America and later died in Florida.

Edith Mary Brown

We'll turn now to Edith. Born in Whitehaven in 1864, her schooling was first at the independent Manchester High School for Girls then at the Croydon High School, also an all-girls independent school. How she came to a personal faith in Christ I have not discovered but from an early age her aspiration was to serve as a medical missionary in India. As we have seen, her older half-sister Mary was already there having married into the Bowden missionary family.

If Edith was to go as a doctor she must first qualify as one but in the 1880s, in spite of being accepted to study in Cambridge, it would not be possible for her as a woman to obtain her medical qualification in England. Her training therefore was done in three different places. She won a scholarship to Girton College, Cambridge, and after graduation in Natural

Sciences in 1885 went first to Exeter to teach science at the Exeter High School for Girls earning money to eventually pay for her medical training. Help came from the Baptist Missionary Society and she was now able to study at the London School of Medicine for Women although had to go to Glasgow to pass the "Scottish Triple Qualification", which she did in 1891. (Interestingly, an 1889 Glasgow press announcement of examination results lists her as "Edith Mary Brown, Whitehaven".)

To tell Edith's story fully would take a book of its own, and it has been told many times. The following paragraphs, therefore, are intended to give just an overview. Once qualified Edith left as quickly as possible for India, working at first with the Baptist Missionary Society. Before long, however, she became so appalled at the state of medical care for women in the country, and especially obstetrics, that within three years she decided to do something about it, and went independent.

With a generous gift from a Christian lady in Bristol she obtained an old schoolhouse and started a Christian medical training centre for women, initially with only four students. To cut a long story short, over the years this developed into the prestigious Christian Medical College in Ludhiana. It would be no exaggeration to say that Edith Brown's work transformed medical services for women both in North India and further afield. In recognition of her work, in the New Year Honours list of 1932 King George V named her a Dame Commander of the Order of the British Empire (DBE). She eventually retired as Principal in 1952 at the age of 88, and lived out her remaining years in Kashmir, dying in December 1956.

Mabel Walther Brown

The third of our Whitehaven Brown missionary ladies is Mabel Walther Brown. I have found little about her early years beyond what is common to the family as a whole. At the 1891 census she was described as a 24-year-old governess, but ten years later she was an assistant teacher at Kings College Civil Service Department, then in 1911 (the family having now moved to Bromley, Kent) she was an Assistant Examiner in the same institution. It would appear that even though Lucy was also at home in Croydon with their mother it was necessary for Mabel to stay close at hand. Like Elizabeth Wilson in our first chapter, her missionary years were delayed until after her mother's death. Very quickly after that event she left for China.

By this time it was 1915 and she was 48 years old when the Brethren assembly at Bromley commended her to take up missionary service. The March 1915 issue of *Echoes of Service* reported: "Mr. and Mrs. M'Alpine expect to set out on their return to Lower Mongolia, with their two children, on March 11th, and two sisters hope to accompany them, in order to join Miss Gates in work at Tu-chia-woa-pu, viz., Miss Mabel W. Brown, commended from Bromley, Kent, and Miss Olive Mae Randall, commended from King's Hall, Willesden Green." (Miss Randall was delayed.)

In May they reached Tatzukow, the city where Mr. & Mrs. M'Alpine planned to settle temporarily to replace a missionary family going on furlough. Miss Kemp had come to meet Mabel and take her the remaining twenty-six miles of her journey to Tu-chia-woa-pu. Caroline Gates, Mabel's more experienced colleague, was a woman of roughly her own age and like her approaching her half century. However, Caroline had been in China for almost thirty years, mostly with the CIM, had been through hard times and was no longer enjoying the strength and stamina she once knew. Had the two of them met before, maybe during her 1905 furlough? It was then that Caroline had come into association with Brethren and returned to China independent of the Mission to work with several other ladies in establishing women's work in the area around Tu-chia-woa-pu.

This was no easy environment. The climate could be rough, with severe windstorms bringing dust from the wide Mongolian steppes. It is clear that Mabel and Caroline worked together well. In a joint letter in early 1916 they described Tu-chia-woa-pu as "one of a good many villages dotted about a small plain surrounded by mountains. It is almost entirely built of mud, and looks very much like a magnified sand village, such as children might try to make on the seashore. ... In the hot weather little naked children play about in the road, and are mud-coloured too. But there are a good many trees in the place, so that, from a little distance, the village has looked quite pretty, with the mountains in the distance behind and fields of grain in front."

There had been a Brethren-style assembly in Tu-chia-woa-pu, Chinese initiated and Chinese led, since the late-1890s. A man from there had arrived in Ping-chuan, eighty miles away, searching for missionaries. Having the gospel explained to him he believed and went back to his home. With the occasional help of visiting missionaries he preached and taught what he had learned and a church was established.

The missionaries had established a school and this was adapted to the seasons as the children were needed to work in the fields at harvest time, plus the daily timetable of village life and patterns of eating varied with the time of year. Children were taught to read the Bible, and on Sundays there was a Sunday School at which the principles of the gospel were taught.

Although the resident population of Tu-chia-woa-pu was Chinese, there were many Mongol people who visited from the areas further north. Reaching them with the message of Jesus was more difficult as many did not speak Chinese and none of the missionaries spoke their Mongolian tongue. For the next seven years, as one of a team of lady missionaries, sometimes three, sometimes four, Mabel taught in the school, ran classes for women in their homes not only in the main village but in the area around. It was steady work week in and week out, summer and winter, often visiting areas to which Caroline had previously been strong enough to go but could not now handle. There were encouragements and disappointments. They kept going, thanking God for those who came to faith in Christ and crying to God for those who gave them much heartache. Back in England her sister Lucy died in May 1918, her death being announced in *Echoes*, described as Mabel's sister and "a member of a devoted missionary family".

Caroline continued to be weak in health, and yet it was Mabel who had to return home first. She came to England for a six-months' furlough in 1920, but set off back to Tu-chia-woa-pu at the end of the year and by mid-1921 was again active in her classes, teaching the phonetic script, on Sundays teaching her women's Bible class, helping with the distribution of grain (as the harvests had failed and there was serious distress), and starting to visit some other villages. Her health, however, refused to hold up, and in early 1922 she went to Peking (Beijing) for a serious operation. Although it was declared successful she was strongly advised to return to England. Caroline Gates accompanied her.

Three years later she went to be with her Lord. As a closing tribute I give the *Echoes of Service* obituary notice in full:

"May 3rd, at Bromley, Kent, MABEL WALTHER BROWN, late of N. China, aged 58. It was after thirty years' waiting that our sister's way opened to the mission-field, but when it did she went, and undertook such work as was possible. After only a few years her health failed, and, though an operation gave temporary cure, she deemed it wise to return to England, in the probability of a recurrence of the disease. This took place, and after ten months' illness she has now gone to be with the Lord. We may remind friends that Echoes Manual, No. 5, dealing with work in Lr. Mongolia, was put together by her out of materials contributed by different labourers. Her whole heart was given to the missionary cause, and she spent much time daily wrestling in prayer for it. The sympathy of our readers will go out towards her only surviving sister, Dr. Edith Brown, of Ludhiana, India."

Thomas Wales & Family
(Kendal to British Guiana)

Thomas Wales was an evangelist, the son of another Thomas Wales, evangelist. He was born at Bow, London in 1855, made a commitment to Christ at an early age and after serving an apprenticeship as a watchmaker struck out himself as a preacher of the Gospel. He was not yet 20 years old when he married Miss Hannah Liller, six years older than himself, in the district of Mile End Old Town in London. The following year, 1875, their first son, Thomas Arthur was born on the Isle of Man.

In 1877 their daughter Louisa Elizabeth (known as "Cissie") was born in West Ham, but by 1881 they were in Ashbourne, Derbyshire where that year's census return has him recorded as a "Scripture Reader", a common term then for an evangelist and colporteur (Bible salesman) in towns around the country. It is not clear exactly what was the pattern of his evangelistic work at this stage.

At the time of the 1881 census they had two children but shortly afterwards a daughter Jane was born, only to die shortly after birth. Jane may in fact have been their second loss of a child as in later years they referred to having had six children, of whom I have been able to find only five.

A pattern of suffering and loss was emerging. Whilst this experience was not uncommon at the time, it was painful nevertheless, and was to colour the rest of their lives. Yet they were able to continue with faith intact. At the birth of Hannah Liller Wales in the autumn of 1882 they were in Highworth, Wiltshire, still moving from place to place.

During 1884 and 1885 they were at Edmonton, Middlesex and initially there was joy. Herbert George Wales was born in the autumn of 1884. The following year, however, was one of seemingly unending tragedy. Firstly 9-yr-old Thomas, next 2-yr-old Hannah and then, not yet one year old, Herbert. Within six months their family of four had been reduced to one. Just 7-yr-old Cissie was left to be the only one who would reach adulthood. The suffering is almost incomprehensible. And yet they went on serving God, who had given but also taken away.

At the 1891 census they are found living in Tottenham, and by this time Thomas was occupied as an itinerant evangelist as distinct from one settled in a specific place. Spending summer months preaching in marquees appears to have been part of his approach; for example in August 1894 he was preaching in a tent at Ludlow.

Just when the sense of God's call to British Guiana developed we don't now know but it could have come, or at least gained strength, from the two or three years the family spent in the very missionary aware assembly at Kendal. What brought them to Kendal is also now unknown but from 1896 to 1898 they lived at no. 6 South Road, and Thomas was engaged in some form of pastoral work in the town in connection with the Brethren assembly. Then in September 1898, long-serving missionary John Rymer wrote from Georgetown of his pleasure that the Wales family would be coming to them. He and his wife urgently needed a break.

Georgetown was no new mission field. There had been an assembly since at least 1840. Mr. Leonard Strong was a former Anglican clergyman expelled from his living in the colony because of his faithful ministry to slaves. Under his early leadership churches had met on what came to be known as Brethren "assembly lines" since even before any did in England. As the nineteenth century drew to a close the assembly in Georgetown by now had around eight hundred in fellowship. Quite apart from further evangelistic outreach there was a major teaching and pastoral leadership demand, and there were other assemblies on the coast and up the rivers.

Into this environment came the three Wales missionaries. Yes, 21-yr-old Cissie was not merely going as her parents' daughter but as a missionary in her own right. They arrived at the Demerara River on the 30th November 1898. Along with nine of the native brethren the existing Georgetown missionary team came out to the boat to meet them: Mr. & Mrs. John Rymer (there since 1879), widowed Mrs. Huntley (since 1857) and one of the three single ladies Miss Elizabeth Baker (since 1888): the other two being Miss Butland (since 1895) and Miss Wakelin (since 1895).

Thomas commented in his first letter home, "Dear Mr. Rymer looks very much worn and tired! I am endeavouring to gather up all the threads of the fabric, so as better to set them free." However "worn and tired" John Rymer may have been it wasn't, though, going to stop this determined Yorkshireman from taking Thomas on an arduous trip up the rivers. He wanted to visit the isolated assemblies once more and to introduce the new missionary before he himself left for the islands and then rest in England. (John Rymer did return to

Guiana, but later contracted a virulent form of leprosy and died in 1907.)

Early Years in Georgetown 1898-1901

It wasn't long before Thomas was busily involved in preaching the gospel. As would be expected in a church of its size Georgetown had a good number of capable preachers, but Thomas had years of experience and was a powerful preacher. Hundreds came to listen to him. Many were pointed to Christ, baptised and came into the church fellowship. And yet there were aspects of the work that disappointed him. There was the East Indian part of the population, speaking Hindi; the Chinese people with their own language, among whom were some Christians. No-one was doing anything much by way of outreach to these people. The same applied to the many Portuguese-speaking people in the area.

He started to preach using interpreters. A group of Chinese Christians was drawn together and he had a faithful interpreter with whom he worked to bring some spiritual food from the Word of God in their own tongue. He was especially touched when one man asked him in very broken English whether it would be possible to bring a Christian teacher over from China to teach them in words they would understand. Thomas frequently mentioned these needs in his reports for *Echoes of Service*, but no-one came.

He was very conscious of the needs of the little churches up the rivers, but it was all too much for one man. He could only go to them very occasionally. Having said that there was a great deal of progress, despite the disappointments that can only be expected among such a large number of people. The local demands in Georgetown were immense, and Hannah developed her own ministry among the womenfolk both in the city and in the villages around.

Cissie was also working alongside Miss Butland to develop a school for the East Indian children, and helping Miss Wakelin with teaching Chinese children, whom she found "very bright". She joined Mrs Huntley on a visit to a leper colony and the elderly lady was deeply impressed at her young companion's ability to speak of Jesus to groups of women in a way that was so loving and clear. Miss Baker described her as "like a sunbeam in the house, always bright and happy, and ready to help anyone". Mrs Huntley wrote of her, "Miss Wales has her heart in the work, and helps in many ways." Miss Wakelin's health had not been good and she was about to leave for England. She was delighted that Cissie would be taking over much of what she had been doing.

Then in mid-April 1900, less than eighteen months after the Wales family arrived in Georgetown the *Echoes of Service* office back in England received a two-word cable message, "Cissie translated". Brief, but they knew what it meant. Thomas and Hannah's one remaining daughter had joined her five brothers and sisters in heaven. As more details arrived they learned than she had started with severe peritonitis. After seventeen days she had ended her short earthly life, of not yet twenty-three years, and gone into the eternal presence of the Saviour she loved and served. Just before she passed away she quietly whispered to her father the words of the Lord Jesus, "Go into all the world and preach the gospel."

The blow to Thomas and Hannah was enormous. Echoing words of Scripture he wrote: "The ways of the Lord are past finding out. He gave to us in all, six children, and now He has them all in His safe keeping. He permitted us to keep this last one for twenty-two and a half years. The Lord gave, and the Lord hath taken away ; blessed be the name of the Lord. In a special sense we feel lonely, yet the Lord sustains us in restful peace in Himself.

The love, too, of these dear people is very touching."

Shortly after this word came from England that Hannah's younger sister had died in London. Thomas wrote again, "This and the previous sorrow, added to her own suffering, cause us grave fears for her health. Her nervous system seems quite shattered. I am sure you will help us in prayer." She did pull round but it was apparent that they needed a change. John Rymer returned from England, and although not so strong as he once was he could pick up much of the responsibility.

St. Vincent 1901-1904

It was mid 1901 before everything was organised. The intention was for Thomas and Hannah to tour several of the West Indian islands, partly for relaxation and at the same time for him to give some pastoral and teaching help to the little assemblies whilst avoiding overstressing himself. This was not the way things materialised.

A severe earthquake and volcanic eruption devastated large areas of St Vincent and they ended up being there for more than two years providing relief and caring in many ways for the suffering people, especially seeking to keep the believers together and encouraged. The poverty was appalling, the physical suffering great. With God-given strength beyond his own he worked furiously through those years. Then in 1904 they returned to England for furlough until late 1905.

Queenstown and Georgetown from 1905

The ministry of Thomas and Hannah during the next thirty years deserves a longer telling but for now we must leave them at this point. After their time in England they initially went to Queenstown, but then returned to Georgetown, serving faithfully together until Hannah passed away in 1935 in her late-80s. She was buried near her daughter. Two years later Thomas went to Australia, and went to his heavenly reward in 1939. Theirs were lives of great suffering, of great faithfulness, and of great blessing to many.

Amy Wharton

(Penrith to India)

The name Wharton had strong connections with the Gospel Hall in Penrith during the later decades of the 19th century and also the first few of the 20th. James Wharton, as we have seen, travelled frequently from Barrow-in-Furness to minister among freed slaves in the United States. He was originally from Penrith. Mr. Thomas Wharton, a prominent tradesman in the town, was active in the Gospel Hall for over thirty years as both an elder and Sunday School Superintendent. He also played a major role in the local YMCA until his death in 1916. Then in 1924 Miss A. E. Wharton went as a missionary to India, serving there until the mid-1950s.

The connection, if any, between James and Thomas has yet to be clarified, but Miss Amy E. Wharton was the second daughter of Thomas and his wife Sarah (née Bell). She was born on 20th April 1888 and the family eventually consisted of four daughters. Amy therefore was brought up in close connection with the Gospel Hall in Queen Street, committed her life to Christ in early years and was also active in the

Penrith branch of the Evangelical Young Women's Christian Association.

Amy was 36 years old by the time she left for India. After her education in local schools she most probably worked for some time in her father's drapery business. Her sisters certainly did. Then in July 1908 aged 20 she left home for nurse training in Scotland. This was firstly in Edinburgh at the Royal Hospital for Sick Children and then from November 1911 at the Western Infirmary, Glasgow, becoming a Charge Nurse before resigning in November 1915. World War 1 led to thousands of young nurses volunteering for Queen Alexandra's Imperial Military Nursing Service. The war was raging, and nurses were needed to care for the sick and wounded. Amy answered that call.

She was at first in the Alexandra Hospital at Cosham, Surrey, caring for injured troops evacuated from the killing fields of France and Belgium. The following year she was granted a discharge to return to Penrith owing to her father's illness but, after his death, was readmitted in the November. Then in April 1917, "Sister Amy Wharton" was decorated with the Royal Red Cross, an award given to a military nurse who has "shown exceptional devotion and competence in the performance of nursing duties, over a continuous and long period, or who has performed an exceptional act of bravery and devotion at her or his post of duty". She received it along with several other nurses at a ceremony with King George V in person.

In August 1917 Amy was posted to Salonika (the Thessalonica of New Testament times) and was there until the war ended. Fighting was at a stalemate, and it has sometimes been said that the major enemy was not the Bulgarians but the mosquitoes. Malaria was rife. Tens of thousands of troops suffered from it, and eventually in September 1918 Amy herself was hospitalised, got well enough to return to work but was again in hospital early the next year, leading to her medical discharge in May 1919.

What was it that then led her to think of missionary service in India? Maybe she'd had this in her mind for many years as a result of the great missionary interest at the Gospel Hall, and visiting missionary speakers. Maybe, as with many other young ladies of the time, her original venture into nursing was intended as preparation for the mission field. Or was it contact with the many Indian troops in Salonika? No record of how she came to be called to missionary service appears to have survived.

Clearly, back in England, her health must have improved. By 1921 she was in Liverpool for further nurse training, this time as a midwife, then in January 1924 the Penrith Observer announced her sailing for India to "take up her work as a medical missionary". She travelled out with a Mr. & Mrs. Young and the plan was that she should at least initially work alongside them, where they had served for the previous twenty years, in the Tinnevelli area of South India.

Anthony Norris Groves had visited the area in the 1830s. Subsequently one of his younger colleagues, an Indian named Arulappan, had seen a great work of the Holy Spirit. There had been thousands of converts and many churches established on simple New Testament lines. Sadly, after his death, a generation or two later most of the Christianity had become little more than nominal. Then in 1895 Handley Bird and Thomas Maynard visited the area.

They found that some of the churches wished for teaching along the lines of Groves and Arulappan and that there was plenty of scope for evangelistic outreach among both the nominally Christian population and the Hindus. Although Anglican, Baptist and American Presbyterian missions had been commenced there were large areas untouched by them. In agreement with the other missions Maynard agreed to concentrate on the north-west part of the district and accepted responsibility for a number of existing village schools.

It was here that Thomas Maynard, bringing his wife and family from their previous base in Coimbatore a hundred miles away (but three hundred by train), began to serve the following year. He named the new mission station Mount Sion, not only a Biblical reference but also after his parents' home back in Tunbridge Wells. Other missionaries arrived and reached out into surrounding areas.

Some of the missionaries whose lives we look at in this book were pioneers, going out into areas far from where the gospel had been preached before. Amy Wharton's ministry was not of that kind. In 1924, almost thirty years on from Maynard's arrival in the district, she was joining an existing group of missionaries in an area where men and women from Brethren assemblies had been active for decades. Amy's first task, though, while stationed with the Youngs at Mount Sion, would be to learn the Tamil language.

From time to time, to gain some familiarity with the locality, she went out into the villages with another missionary, especially with Miss

Minna Noschke. She was a young nurse of Anglo-German extraction, born and brought up in London with a German father and English mother. She had been in India since 1921 and apart from furloughs was to be there until the 1960s.

Amy's first term of service lasted six years until in 1930 she returned to England on furlough. Once she was reasonably comfortable with the language she could get more involved not only with local outreach at Mount Sion but in the villages around. In July 1925 she wrote of a group of villages that "were first opened to us through the medical work. Miss Noschke has been visiting them several times."

After a year or so she is found working at Vadamalapuram, and this is where the majority of her work was to be done for the next twenty years.

Vadamalapuram, eighteen miles from Mount Sion, had been first mentioned by *Echoes of Service* in a letter dated December 1904. It would appear that there had been previous visits to the place and that there had been some success. It was seen as a promising future location, there being over sixty villages within little more than a five mile radius.

In December 1903 Miss Mary Wright wrote: "Miss Aldwincklc and Miss Vernêde had a good time with the people at Vadamalapuram a few days ago, the Lord blessing the Word. A day school has been opened, and several boys have joined. Miss Vernêde and I are looking to the Lord to guide as to whether He would have us go there as soon as the place is ready to live in."

It was actually a single male missionary, Frank Rose, who first went to live there in mid-1904 and built the bungalow that would house missionaries for many years. He had with him an Indian school-teacher and an experienced Indian preacher and the work developed.

When Amy arrived here in 1926 there was a medical clinic. As a highly experienced nurse she was to carry much of the responsibility for this. There was a thriving educational work with day pupils, and also a sizeable boarding school. Caring for the children was also to be a significant part of her role. She would also join in evangelistic trips into the villages, and these were often the main subject of her letters, even more than the associated dispensary work.

This was not the kind of high profile missionary work seen in some other places with lots of variety, travel and excitement. No, this was hard slog, week in, week out, month in, month out. Consistency, determination, patience, often with little to show for some time. And yet, blessing did flow, especially in the lives of the young.

Back home for furlough in Penrith, in November 1929 she was called on to describe her activities in India and open the annual sale of work at the Evangelical YWCA. She had intended to be back in Vadamalapuram by the end of 1930 but it was January 1931 before she returned. In late-1930 the Penrith Observer again reports her as describing her work, this time to the Missionary Study Class at her home church, the Gospel Hall on Queen Street.

Back in India the work of the clinic continued, although this was always seen as a means to an end, a way of getting in contact with people, rather than an end in itself. During the whole of Miss Wharton's ministry it never grew to a large scale, remaining as a nurse-led clinic and never having capacity for more than three in-patients at a time. Only after her retirement was the boarding school moved to another village so that the accommodation could be used as a somewhat larger hospital with a resident doctor.

There were frequent encouragements during these years, with both boys and girls professing faith in Christ, and also adults. Amy took on responsibility for the Sunday School at

Vadamalapuram, and this was a fruitful ministry. Another lady missionary had moved away leaving several monthly meetings for Christian women in the villages to be looked after so she added these to her programme.

The challenges were many. One very significant difficulty was the caste system. It was not always easy to get either adults or young people to accept that as human beings they were all equal before God. They were often not prepared to sit together in the same classes or services. A young low-caste boy was once found in tears; he had been beaten for getting too close to higher caste children. It was often seen as a spiritual triumph when an adult lady would sit together and listen to the Gospel along with lower caste women.

Idolatry was a further challenge. Like the Thessalonian believers in apostolic times there were those who "turned to God from idols to worship the living and true God" (1 Thess. 1:9) but this was often a difficult hurdle. Another issue was alcohol and drunkenness, especially with the younger men given easy availability of "toddy", made from fermented juice of the palm tree. But with constant prayer the work continued and the number of believers increased.

During the years 1936-39 Amy appears to have been back in England for an extended period. I have not as yet been able to establish the reason for this, but can't help wondering whether it was a matter of health. In view of her wartime experiences at Salonica with repeated malaria, it may be that she needed to spend some time away from the tropical environment. However, before the start of the 2nd World War, now in her early fifties, she was back in India and stayed there for seven years throughout the hostilities until taking a further furlough in 1946/7.

During these years the extracts from her letters published in Echoes of Service mention more of the medical work than previously, including the scourge of leprosy. The spiritual challenges, however, were not ignored. Caste continued to be a major issue. One teenage girl, for example, was taken away from the hospital by her mother because she would be too close to lower caste women and girls.

Her final years in India were not at Vadamalapuram but where she first started thirty years before, at Mount Sion, then at the end of 1953 Amy returned to England and by March was back in Penrith for a furlough, living with her sisters in the old family home. Her hope had been to return to India for at least another three years but this was not to be.

Her eldest sister Edith became seriously ill and Amy felt the need to be with her but by late 1955 she was again thinking of returning to the field.. In the meantime she was helping Mrs. Winter with the women's work at the Gospel Hall in Penrith.

When Edith died in 1956, however, other circumstances arose in the family, including another bereavement. She was once again delayed. How she longed to get back to India. Time and again she began to plan her return but each time it proved impossible. She was, though, pleased to have a good number of opportunities to speak at various meetings around Cumbria to stir up interest in the country.

She spoke of going back to the Tamil country although not to Vadamalapuram but to a place called Mangalapuram. She and her friend Miss Elsie Phillipson, who was already back in India, had talked of working together but Amy just wanted to do what was God's will, and that seemed to be, for the present at least, to stay in Penrith. Her friend Dorothy Fisk (of Morocco; see later chapter) who was currently staying with her parents nearby in Penrith, advised her to stay and she took that as confirmation of what she increasingly had felt to be best.

Living in the lovely family home on the hillside above Penrith Amy could have been seen as financially secure, but it was definitely a case of "asset rich, cash poor" and there were some difficult times. Her ageing sisters were struggling with their drapery business in town, and Amy herself was having difficulty getting an old age pension. When that problem was solved she rejoiced in gratitude to God for what seemed to be a remarkable change of official attitude toward her.

She lived on with her surviving sisters for many years, but never forgot South India, corresponding with many workers there.

Her widowed sister Olive died in 1968 then in 1975 her last surviving sister Ivy. Not long afterwards Amy went to live in the assemblies' Eventide Home in Southport. She went from there to her reward on the last day of March 1981, in her 93rd year. She was buried at Southport, very close to the author's own mother who just a few years before had spent her closing years in the same care home.

It is in no sense a negative comment to say that Amy Wharton's missionary career appears not in any sense to have been one of high profile individual achievement. Rather it is a story of steady collaborative working, both in nursing care and evangelistic outreach, among the people to whom she believed God had sent her. She was building on foundations already laid by others. All too often such unspectacular work goes unknown and forgotten, but not by God.

John, Edith & Grace Rotherie

(Whitehaven & Carlisle to Trinidad)

John Rothery was born on the 26th December 1892 at Whitehaven. It has not been easy to pinpoint information about his early years due to other young men named John Rothery being in the area at around the same time. However, he was educated at the Whitehaven Grammar School and then trained as a teacher. As to his spiritual background he trusted Christ as his Saviour at the age of 12 and would later describe himself as having been profoundly influenced by the example of a godly father.

By the time he was in his early twenties he had moved around the country, and it was in 1915 at Steyning, Sussex, now 22 years old, he married a young lady five or six years older than himself, by the name of Edith Danston.

In the records of the Parish Church, Kingston by Sea, Sussex, John is described as a "2nd Lieutenant 15th Battalion Royal Fusiliers". Four years earlier at the 1911 census Edith was recorded as a Salvation Army Officer in Darwen, Lancashire. Was the location of the marriage determined by her now serving in the Steyning area or by his being stationed there with the army?

Edith had been born in Northamptonshire, and her family appears to have maintained a presence in that county. For many years when she and John returned from Trinidad on furlough it was in Wellingborough near Northampton that they made their home until their return to the mission field.

Following the war they settled in Whitehaven, and in the 1921 census John was recorded as having a drapery business at 62 Lowther Street, with Edith as his assistant. Whether after that they moved south for a while is uncertain but it was in London that they were both baptised by immersion in 1926. However, it was from Whitehaven that in the early 1930s they were commended for missionary service.

John, now 37, had felt a call to serve God in the West Indies. He had taken an interest in the work of a Miss Millington who many years before had given up her shop in Church Street, Burnley to take the gospel to the women and children of St. Vincent. As he planned to move forward he consulted the elders in the Whitehaven assembly. They backed him in his aspiration, assuring him of the full fellowship of the church. His plan was for an exploratory visit of six months, for this first trip leaving Edith in Whitehaven.

We next find John on a ship to Trinidad, accompanying evangelist Albert Widdison (father of the later evangelist Phil Widdison, well known in Cumbria) who was on a trip to conduct Gospel campaigns on the island. John appears to have left Mr. Widdison at some point to explore other areas of the island and found his way to San Fernando in the south west.

By the time he returned home he was convinced that God wanted them on Trinidad. Furthermore he had a sense of where on the island. There was a strong missionary presence already, and had been since the later years of the previous century, closely associated with work in neighbouring British Guiana. (See our chapter on Thomas Wales.) There were several assemblies in existence, but most of the work was with the West Indian population.

Whilst not wanting to isolate from the other missionaries whose work was chiefly West Indian, he felt his call was toward the "East Indians", people who had come to Trinidad to work on the sugar plantations from India, and were therefore of quite distinct racial, cultural, religious and linguistic background from the majority Afro-Caribbean population. At the time there were well over a hundred thousand East Indians on the island. Hinduism and Islam were their two main religions, and Hindi their most common language. Many did not speak English.

Back in England one of John's early priorities was to find someone to teach him Hindi so that he could go at least partly prepared. He set about finding someone to help him with this and also in October 1932 started a six-month course at the School of Missionary Medicine in London. In August 1933 John and Edith boarded at Dover a ship bound for the West Indies. This was to be the first of many such voyages over the next thirty years.

Within their first three months they had found a small hall to rent for meetings and gathered together four Indian Christians. In early November they broke bread for the first time - just six people, two Indian men, two Indian women, and themselves. One of the men was anxious to help by teaching Hindi.

It was not long before opposition came. One of the rumours spread was that John would be paid £10 (about £600 at today's values) for every person that they baptised. Many other slanderous details they never knew and decided simply to ignore it all and get on with the work. Gradually confidence was built.

The response to open air preaching was extremely surprising. Between two and three hundred would stand and listen for well over an hour. When they started to hold indoor preaching services twenty people came to the first one, but the second week there were a hundred. Some of the preaching was in English, some in Hindi.

A mid-week meeting was started, with addresses on subjects such as the Sonship and deity of Christ, aimed at the better educated among the Muslim men. Numbers rose to over a hundred, then a hundred and fifty. The Sunday School was growing, and Edith's weekday sewing class for girls quickly had to be split into two as the numbers passed a hundred and sixty. Many were showing signs of a spiritual awakening. It seemed as though the Rotheries had arrive in San Fernando just as (to use the words of Jesus) the fields were ripe and ready to be harvested.

A new hall was needed to accommodate the growing work and this became John's big project. In July 1936, less than three years from their arrival on the island, the new building was opened, believers from around the island coming in hundreds for the inaugural conference, also with Gospel preaching and baptisms. The impact locally was considerable, and importantly the permanence of a building gave the lie to one of the accusations that had circulated, that the missionaries would not be staying long but would soon be gone.

Then quite suddenly in 1937 the climate changed. Hatred of the "White Man" overflowed onto the streets and the missionaries had to cope with the vilest of insults and threats. This was not an easy period but the work went quietly and steadily on. It indeed provided an opportunity to hand over more responsibility to the native brethren while the missionaries stayed away from the limelight. Gradually the atmosphere calmed.

This had in fact been John's aim from the start, to build up the converts so that they could take the lead. He had no wish to be the kind of missionary on whom the local church would always be dependent, and this became a major theme of his ministry over the following years.

Having returned to the U.K. for a 1938 furlough he and Edith then found it quite difficult to get back across the Atlantic. They did, however, manage to sail in June 1940 (not without its dangers!) and were able to continue their work through the war years.

In 1939 John had spoken at a meeting in Carlisle, and in the congregation was a young lady, Grace Armstrong. In later years Grace spoke of how at that meeting she felt strongly drawn towards joining the the work in Trinidad, but several years elapsed before she was able to go. However, in 1944, with German U-boats still patrolling the Atlantic, she boarded a ship at Glasgow for her first crossing.

Edith Rothery now had Grace's help in the activities she ran for women and children. Many years after her retirement, when Grace was back on the island for a visit, people would stop her in shops and in the street to thank her for the help she had given to them in their youth, and in particular encouraging them to faith in Christ.

John's work continued to be focused chiefly on the East Indian population in San Fernando, but there were also several other assemblies in the south of the island and he would frequently visit these for Bible teaching. Edith and Grace would also help there in meetings for women. They had at least two furloughs in the late-1940s and mid-1950s. During the latter Edith and Grace came to England while initially John went on a speaking tour in North America.

The years went by, and as had been John's aspiration from the start the local assemblies were increasingly able to stand on their own feet without needing the presence of a missionary. Edith died in April 1960 at the age of 73. Her funeral service, which was attended by hundreds from all over Trinidad, was taken by evangelist Fred Whitmore who was visiting from England to conduct gospel campaigns on the island.

The following year John Rothery and Grace Armstrong were married, and they continued the work together for another six years before in 1967 retiring to England, happy that they were leaving churches in good hands.

Back in England John and Grace settled in Worthing and he quickly began to be called upon for preaching and teaching around the south of England and further afield. In Whitehaven years afterwards the late Edmund Messenger remembered, "As young men we used to love to sit and listen to him. He was a real teacher."

After a period of illness John passed away peacefully in his sleep at a Worthing nursing home on New Year's Day 1975 at the age of 82. For him it was truly a "new year" as he went to meet the Saviour whom he had served for so long. The service at Bedford Row Evangelical Church was led by Mr. A. Pulleng.

Grace, almost twenty years younger than John, lived on for another thirty-five years continuing to help for as long as she could in the Worthing assembly activities and also with work for the blind in the local area. She died in May 2010 at the age of 96, leaving instructions that she should be buried with "no tombstone or memorial to mark my grave."

Eric & Dorothy Fisk

(Carlisle and Penrith to Morocco)

On a damp, chilly February morning in 1926 a crowd of farmers from many miles around gathered at Braithwaite Hall Farm, about half way between Penrith and Carlisle. Word had got around that the livestock on sale that morning was of good quality. The owner was retiring and all must be sold. Unusually, the retiring farmer was only 30 years old and had worked this land for less than three years, but was known for having transformed an almost derelict farm into a desirable property. Who was he? Why and where was he going so soon?

Eric

His name was Eric Gibson Fisk. As a Captain in the King's Own Royal Lancaster Regiment he had served with distinction during the 1914-18 War, being awarded the Military Cross twice. Having been severely wounded at the Battle of Cambrai in late-1917 he had spent years in hospital, sometimes not expected to live, and going through more than a dozen operations. The army had then arranged a programme of agricultural training for him, sending him to work with a Cumbrian yeoman farmer, and in 1923 he had bought this 173 acre farm.

During Eric's years in Cumberland he had also become known for travelling around the county on his motorcycle preaching at a variety of churches and mission halls. Not only that but he held services in his farmhouse kitchen, and many came to them. He met John Laing, the Carlisle builder (later Sir John Laing, CBE) who introduced him to the Brethren assembly at Hebron Hall. At one hamlet where he preached regularly people came to Christ and John Laing provided a building in which meetings continued for many years following.

Although not a Cumberland man by origin Eric's connections to the county, and to Penrith especially, were to become very strong. He was born at Bebbington on the Wirral in 1895 the son of Edward and Ellen Fisk. His father, a commercial traveller, sadly died when Eric was only 10 years old and his mother then for some years ran a boarding house in Wallasey. He was converted to Christ in 1913 and became an officer in the Boys' Brigade and active in the Field Road Mission, Wallasey. His mother moved to live in Cumberland and his older sister Kathleen was in 1928 to become the wife of George Winter of Penrith, widely known as a preacher throughout Cumberland and Westmorland.

Eric had wanted to be a missionary since before the war, to take the message of God's love in Christ to people who had never heard it. Leaving the farm, his plan now for the early summer of 1926 was to join in a gospel outreach at Bowness on Windermere alongside evangelist John M'Alpine. From there he would head for France to do language study before leaving for missionary service in North Africa, something he was doing with the commendation of the church at Hebron Hall, and with the encouragement also of the Gospel Hall, Penrith.

He was, however, to acquire an even stronger connection to the town. When he sailed in a missionary group from Southampton to Tangier in October 1926 his home address on the passenger list was Beech Grove, Penrith. This was also given as the home address of one of the young ladies in the group, Miss Dorothy Margaret Smith. Five months later, 25th March 1927, they were to marry in Casablanca.

Dorothy

Beech Grove on Lowther Street was the Smith family home in Penrith. It was a godly home and from an early age Dorothy went with them to the Gospel Hall on Queen Street. Eric once wrote that his wife's parents always ended each day of their lives by saying together the

Doxology: *Praise God, from whom all blessings flow.* In later life, when there were problems over support for the North African Arabic Bible project the Smiths out of their own means provided a substantial proportion of the translation costs. For many years they ran a Sunday School in a nearby village, and Mrs. Smith led a girls' Bible class. Dorothy trusted Christ in her early years. Even from the age of twelve she knew she was going to be a missionary, and taught her first Sunday School class at fourteen.

Her father, Mr. J. W. Smith, O.B.E., was Clerk to the Penrith Rural District Council, at the time the largest local government unit of its type in the country. Today he would be known as Chief Executive. Originally from Gravesend in Kent he occupied this position for many decades becoming nationally known for some of his developmental initiatives.

Three years younger than Eric, Dorothy had been born in June 1898 and was her parents' only child. Following her education, on the outbreak of war she served as an assistant in her father's office from August 1914. This was a time when women were called on to fill positions previously occupied men who were now going off to the trenches. Initially she volunteered simply to help out for a few months (the war was not expected to last long!) but ended up serving there throughout the war years, becoming his chief assistant, described later as "most capable ... thoroughly acquainted with the work of every department". In 1918 she volunteered her resignation so as not to continue occupying a position that could be filled by a man returning from the forces. The Council refused her resignation and persuaded her to continue until July 1921 when (by now 23 years of age) she left, once again feeling the obligation to leave a space for a returned serviceman.

Press reports in April of the following year refer to Miss Smith receiving a "Special Commendation" voted unanimously by the Council, and seemingly organised by the Chairman to the total surprise of her father, honouring her outstanding service and "special wartime duties". To use the Chairman's words she "during the greater part of the war undertook very onerous and important duties ... with zeal and ability". Sadly, the reports do not give details of what these duties were, although one councillor mentioned having had "a good deal of association with Miss Smith in connection with food and coal control". These special duties were to be listed on an inscribed copy of the Council resolution and presented to her as a mark of their appreciation and esteem.

And so, Miss Dorothy Smith left Penrith for Liverpool to train at the Royal Southern Hospital and was first registered as a nurse in 1925. Midwifery training followed at Queen Charlotte's Hospital, London. During her absences in Liverpool and London her parents had come to know the young Captain Eric Fisk and so she met her husband to be.

Early Years in Morocco

For the first year or so Eric and Dorothy worked with the North African Mission in Casablanca, but gradually became more exercised in mind about the remoter areas. In early 1928 Eric wrote: "As there are a number of workers in Casablanca we felt our field of service lay where Christ has not yet been named. Whilst we were looking to the Lord for guidance, we received an invitation to open work amongst the Soussy Berbers on the frontiers of their country, which is at present closed to Europeans. We are building a wee mud house adjoining a native inn a day's journey from Marrakech. Some Christian friends have rented the inn, and are giving us land to build a little native house. We hope to do dispensary work and sell Scriptures, and extend as the way opens." From this time onward they worked independently of any missionary society whilst maintaining Christian fellowship with workers in many.

Dorothy rapidly became adequately fluent in Arabic and was able to commence her dispensary work at an early stage. People came to her from a wide area, including tribes people from the mountain areas although with them it was often a struggle due to their non-Arabic language. Eventually they started to do tours into the mountains and longed to be able to communicate the gospel of Christ to these people on whom Islam had been imposed by threat of the sword.

More locally they started to set up small outlying clinic rooms which they could visit periodically. Eric went out to markets to distribute Gospels to those who could read, to explain them to those who would listen, and to set up a Bible shop (but permission from the French authorities was not immediately forthcoming). He started a regular Bible Class for Moslem men, as well as preaching during the clinic sessions, and many were very interested. Dorothy had a weekly afternoon class for their wives.

In December 1932 Eric could write of God's faithfulness. "In our work out here we can testify to the wonderful faithfulness of our God.

It takes money to carry on our medical work (which of course is free), and when we need fresh supplies He always sends the necessary help. Through our own experience and the advice of some of the elder missionaries on the field, we are now nicely equipped and able to deal with most of the dreadful diseases prevalent in this land."

In 1935 they wrote of baptisms, but one of the challenges faced was the predicament of young Christian girls. Their Moslem parents, under Islamic law, could compel them to marry any man whom they chose for them. Eric sometimes could negotiate a delay until a suitable Christian man could be found but it was rarely successful as there was not an adequate supply. Some, however, continued to maintain bright Christian testimonies even within their Moslem homes.

Numbers of conversions and baptisms continued to increase, but they had to be wary. The size of the new Christian fellowship increased, eventually in later years growing into a genuinely Moroccan local church of around forty while many others had moved away to other areas taking the gospel with them. It began to be noticed and spies were sometimes detected, attempting to identify the believers and to find ways of accusing them.

Being a Christian convert in an Islamic environment is far from easy, and far from physically safe.

There was opposition, which Eric described in his book *The Cross Versus The Crescent*, but there were also encouragements. For many years it became possible to host annual residential conferences for both missionaries and national believers, at which there could be over a hundred and fifty people present for fellowship around the Word of God and the Communion of bread and wine.

In 1937 Dorothy came back to Penrith in preparation for the birth of their second child, a daughter Irene born in the December, their son David having been born some years earlier. Eric followed her home later, and the work was left in the hands of good friends who had been living long-term in Morocco for business reasons and had been the instigators humanly speaking of the Fisks' initial move out from Casablanca.

After a six months furlough Eric was back in Morocco by June 1938 and Dorothy followed with the baby in September. The following year they enjoyed a visit from two Penrith ladies, Miss Howe and Miss Hodgson. Dorothy referred to this in an address to Penrith's evangelical YWCA in 1940.

New Cumbrian Workers, but now the War

In 1938 Cumbria provided two more recruits for Morocco in the persons of 29-yr-old Harry Ratcliffe from Keswick and 20-yr-old Tom Frears from the Woodhouse assembly, Whitehaven. They were to have accompanied Eric but for some reason he was delayed so the two of them sailed together regardless to Tangier in October, and Eric followed the next month.

Both Harry and Tom were to become long-term missionaries, after the war taking back with them to Morocco their new Cumbrian wives. In 1946 Tom Frears returned to Whitehaven and married Dorothy Ashbridge. They went together to Morocco the following year and served together until 1983. Christina Taylor from Westfield Gospel Hall, Workington in 1950 became Mrs. Ratcliffe and they served until retiring back to Whitehaven in 1980. It was Harry Ratcliffe who in 1986 was to give the funeral address for Dorothy Fisk in Carlisle. Sadly their stories will have to wait for a later paper.

In March 1940 Eric wrote of the orphanage they'd opened a previous year and was positive about the future. However, war intervened and by July they and many other missionaries were back home in England. Harry Ratcliffe and Tom

Frears however, both single men, stayed on in the international city of Tangier.

It was not until January 1945 that *Echoes* was able to announce that "Mr. E. G. Fisk has safely reached Morocco". In April he was reporting that the believers were meeting faithfully together again, some coming long distances despite provisions being so scarce that "it is impossible to provide then with even a cup of tea". The school and orphanage had been closed down during the war, but now a Sunday School was restarted, and the clinic was reopened to the best of his ability and resources. Back in Penrith Dorothy and her mother were busy sorting all kinds of goods that had been sent them for onward transmission to Morocco. And so the work began to rebuild. Dorothy returned in December.

During 1947 and 1948 Dorothy was back at home in Penrith for much of the time. In August 1948 Eric also returned but in the December they returned to the field together. Little mention is made of the children in their published letters but it is possible that they were largely brought up by their grandparents in Penrith, this being a not unusual arrangement at the time although during the war years they would have had both parents there with them. I must now, however, skip over a few years to come to what was possibly Eric Fisk's greatest legacy, the North African Arabic Bible.

The 1950s and Bible Translation

The Bible had been available in classical Arabic for centuries but in Morocco this cultured language was not intelligible to the bulk of the population. Over the previous three hundred years the influence of Portuguese, Spanish and more recently French had altered the speech of the people, and in addition there was overlap with the Berber tribal dialects. The New Testament in Moroccan Arabic had been available for some years, but only small parts of the Old Testament.

Eric and other missionaries were very aware of the need for a whole Bible in dialect that would be understood by the ordinary Moroccan reader. This became his central focus, but was far from straightforward. With Moroccan helpers called Salim and Henry (plus a team of missionary colleagues at a distance, and meeting occasionally) he worked often eight hours a day for weeks on end, from Genesis to Revelation replacing classical vocabulary and phraseology that would be understood in the east in Algeria and Tunisia but unintelligible in Morocco. Moroccan dialect colloquial Arabic was used, remaining true to the original biblical meaning while being more "friendly" to a Moroccan ear. At last a manuscript was ready to show to the publishers.

Then came a blow. Discussions with the British & Foreign Bible Society hit a serious hitch. The Society had concluded that there would not be sufficient demand in Morocco to justify the publication. Whilst certainly unhappy at some of the economic logic of the Bible Society management Eric had to accept that a "Union" Bible for the three countries should be the objective. He must start all over again at Genesis and, with Henry and a few colleagues, produce something usable across the whole region even if not universally acceptable in every detail. This would call for compromise on all sides.

Easier said than done! Algerian and Tunisian workers, both native and expatriate, at first mocked the idea; to them Moroccan Arabic was too "corrupted". Overly Moroccan sounding words and phrases were taken out and drafts were circulated. Even more was wanted out by the countries to the east, whilst the drafts would come back from Moroccan workers with their favourite local expressions written back in.

This was a period of great stress, with Eric in the middle between conflicting demands and strong personalities, among whom he himself was undoubtedly one. Longstanding relationships were damaged during those years. Without a doubt he was not always a model of diplomacy, but he was fighting for what he believed was his God-given closing work, and was determined to achieve a North African Arabic Bible that was usable in all the three countries.

Eventually the work was done, its principles endorsed by the BFBS against some residual opposition across the region. Sir John Laing had helped in relationships with the Society. Eric had been building up a publication fund gradually over the years from many different sources large and small, and now on 22nd June 1960 as the manuscript was handed over to the BFBS in London Sir John added to that generously.

To tell this story in detail would take far more space than we have available here, and maybe some of it would be less than spiritually nourishing. At times the Devil was sowing discord between God's servants, but he could not stop the work.

Furthermore, at one crucial period Dorothy was taken seriously ill and endured many long weeks of suffering in a woefully inadequate and clinically indisciplined hospital with only one qualified nurse, and Eric himself having to provide much of the nursing care.

Despite all the ups and downs God brought them through to a conclusion, the result was achieved, and in 1960 during a weekly prayer meeting of the North African Mission the first copies arrived. It was subsequently viewed by Arabic scholars as a superb work. In recognition of this achievement Eric was made an Honorary Life Governor of the British & Foreign Bible Society.

Closing Years

After the ending of the French Protectorate and the return of the Moroccan Sultan the work of missionaries became more challenging. For native Christians who had converted from Islam it was often even more difficult and some paid with their lives, accused of "apostasy" as well as trumped up charges that could be twisted to mean "blasphemy".

Through the Bible translation period Eric and Dorothy tried to live as quietly as possible within the Jewish quarter of a larger city where they would be less obtrusive and not subject to continual spying. Eventually, though they had to retire and in 1966, with Eric now aged 71 they moved to Malta, hoping occasionally to be able to visit Morocco from there.

After short time, however, Dorothy's health was giving concern and they decided to move back to England. Then Eric became ill, went through an unsuccessful operation and suffered for over two years before he passed away to his heavenly reward in October 1969. He was buried in Southampton. Leith Samuel, son of Eric's very earliest Christian friend on Merseyside, officiated.

Dorothy moved north to Carlisle, living with her daughter Irene, enjoying the fellowship of the Morton Park assembly there, today remembered as a rather frail little lady. She became increasingly blind, suffered a severe stroke and after some difficult years passed away in February 1986 at the age of 87.

Joyce Shackley

(Workington to Sabah & Korea)

Joyce Shackley was commended to missionary service in Borneo from the Gospel Hall, Corporation Road, Workington, in 1961. She was almost 30 years old and had been conscious of her call to overseas service for some years but was unable to respond immediately due to her being needed at home to support her ailing mother until her death in August 1960. Once, as a very young woman, at the end of a challenging indoor gospel service led by Open Air Mission evangelists at the Gospel Hall she went forward to the front of the hall with others who were confessing their faith for the first time. Her friend could not quite understand this as surely Joyce had trusted the Lord long before. The explanation was her sense of a further call to serve.

Joyce came from a family deeply rooted in the history of the Open Brethren movement in West Cumbria. Her maternal grandfather had been one of the group who organised the building of the hall on Corporation Road, and was also the contractor who built it. He had been actively involved in the assembly as a young man long before that. At a time during the 1880s when the local authority was attempting to hinder the Salvation Army and the Brethren from preaching in the open air Robert Bragg was one of those in court.

Joyce's mother, Leah, was the youngest daughter in Robert's large family She was born in 1894 and in 1922 married Walter Shackley, the youngest son of another large family. He grew up in Harrington his father Joseph Shackley having been a builder and manager of the local sewage works who sadly died when Walter was only three years old. Although not much is now known about him it is recorded that Joseph had early contact with Brethren and as a 20-yr-old had been in lodgings with a family active in the Whitehaven assembly.

After their marriage Walter and Leah at first lived in Harrington and were members of the fellowship at the Workington Gospel Hall. He must have been seen by the elders as a very promising younger man, as in May 1927 when he was only thirty years old he was invited to join them in the oversight of the church. Later, however, he and Leah set up home in Cockermouth where Walter now had his employment. Joyce was born ten years into their marriage. An earlier boy had died in infancy so that Joyce became effectively their only child. It was in the Cockermouth assembly that Joyce had her first experiences of church life in younger years.

Joyce was baptised by immersion in Workington at the age of eighteen on 25th September 1950, one of a group of ten including her cousin Miss Betty Mawson who as Mrs. Stannard (Joyce's closest surviving relative) is still today the assembly organist. Some of this group were from Workington, while three including Joyce and Betty were from Cockermouth although around this time due to people moving from the area Joyce was left as only one of two younger people in the Cockermouth assembly. As a consequence her formative years were spent largely with older people and it has to be said that she was seen as somewhat "old fashioned".

Then in her mid-twenties her father's health and change of employment led to a move to Workington. They lived on Corporation Road just along from the Gospel Hall where the assembly had a strong missionary interest with annual missionary conferences and year-round systematic financial support to many overseas workers.

Joyce has been described in Workington as "a most unlikely missionary". She was quiet and unassuming, not the thrusting energetic type of person at all. Conventional wisdom was that those suitable for overseas work would already have proved themselves in Christian activity at home. Joyce hadn't even taught a Sunday School class, but she knew she had been called to go.

British North Boneo (later renamed Sabah)

Unfortunately the Gospel Hall elders' minute book, normally very systematic since early in the century, has a five year gap from 1959 to 1964 - except for one item, a page describing preparations for Joyce's farewell event on 9th September. There is no surviving record of her application for commendation to missionary work or of the elders' thoughts about this development. What is very clear, though, is that they they were convinced of her call, supported her desire to go, and gave her a warm send-off assuring her that the prayers of the church would follow her. In 1961 she left Workington for what was then British North Borneo to join a group of existing missionaries. Also new to the field at the same time were Mr. & Mrs. Boyd Aitken with whom she travelled.

Mr. & Mrs. Fred Pucknell had been in China as missionaries for almost thirty years when they had to leave following the communist takeover. In common with many other China missionaries they now looked at other countries with a substantial Chinese population. Along with the younger Mr. & Mrs. George Hanlon they felt drawn toward North Borneo and in early 1951 the two brethren went to do a survey of the needs and opportunities. This led to their settling there, initially together in Tenom and after a while the Pucknells in Jesselton (Kota Kinabalu).

In May 1955 the Echoes of Service magazine published a full page article by Fred Pucknell about North Borneo, this following a lengthier article in the previous year's 4th quarter issue of Echoes Quarterly Review. Were these the means by which Joyce Shackley's interest in Borneo was stirred? It would not be surprising and it is known that over the next few years she corresponded with Mrs. Pucknell.

While the Borneo Evangelical Mission had been working in other areas with indigenous tribes little evangelistic work had been done among the tens of thousands of the Chinese population. Permission from the Governor was now obtained to work among Chinese-speaking people only, although later this was expanded to include English speakers who included many from the Indian subcontinent.

Work with Emmaus Bible courses was very successful and gradually some came to faith in Christ. Tenom had a visit in 1955 from a

Chinese evangelist from Malaya, and there were several conversions. It was realised that many of the scattered farms run by the Hakka Chinese had a gramophone, so gospel recordings were distributed with Chinese preaching and music.

After returning from a furlough the Hanlons extended their house in Tenom (a wooden structure on stilts to protect against flooding. By 1958 it was now suitable also as schoolroom for their children and for meetings of the small church including a Sunday School of almost 100 children.

The work in both places was developing, and at the end of the year came reinforcement in the form of David Smith, commended from Dalkeith near Edinburgh, while also from Scotland in mid-1959 came Miss Betty Dennison. The little assembly at Tenom had grown to sixteen. In Jesselton there were around fifty believers and now Mr. & Mrs. Geoffrey Bull were coming to take over from the Pucknells as they went for furlough in Australia. David Smith and Elizabeth Dennison were married in Jesselton and settled in Tenom.

It was into this missionary environment that Joyce Shackley arrived in October 1961, the work well started but with much remaining to be done.

Nine Years in Tenom, Sabah

On 21st October 1961 Mrs. Hanlon had come to Jesselton to meet Joyce, and after a welcome meeting on the first evening they took the train ("very slow, ten miles per hour") to Tenom while the Aitkens remained in Jesselton. At Tenom there was another welcome meeting, and it included around forty young people which must have been a great encouragement. Her first home was was with the Hanlons and her first task was to learn Hakka Chinese. Her first teacher was a young sister from the assembly, and she used a training manual developed by the China Inland Mission. One feature of this was its emphasis on as quickly as possible learning to read the Bible, her first challenge being chapters 1 to 3 of John's Gospel. By early January she could read the first 21 verses but doubted her ability to pass her first examination in April.

Although Joyce was careful not to claim much ability with the language those who knew her say that she did in fact become very competent. This was helped, after a while living in the Hanlons' home, by living over a shop beside a Chinese family, this giving her day-to-day interaction with both young and old. Her Christian witness also had an impact for good in this family. She is still remembered fondly.

In addition to Tenom itself the missionaries reached out to the Chinese in the more rural areas, including travel by dugout canoe across crocodile-infested rivers and long hot tramps through the tropical mud.

Many of the people had their small plots of land or were employed on the rubber plantations. They were very poor, Joyce wrote. "They live in terrible hovels, it has almost to be seen to be believed." And yet among these people there were some who had come to faith in Christ and would sit under their houses (on stilts due to repeated flooding) to listen to the teaching and to sing God's praise. There were three assemblies, one of them thirty miles away, and other meetings in homes.

Gradually she became sufficiently fluent to speak and teach herself. The Chinese parents and children valued education. Good relationships had been established with the headmasters of quite a number of schools, and Joyce would go out along the muddy roads to these primitive classrooms to teach English as the last lesson of an afternoon and follow it with a voluntary Bible lesson in Sunday School style.

In addition to the regular activities of the assembly in town, with Sunday school, young people's meetings, women's meetings and more, this became Joyce's main work which she carried out faithfully. She had grit and stickability in what could be difficult circumstances. She was noted for being quite relaxed about driving a battered old Land Rover on the muddy, often flooded roads. "If I get stuck, there's always someone will come along to help." In one word she has been described as a "character".

Joyce was extremely reticent in talking about herself and what she did. Back in Workington during her first furlough she spoke at the women's session of the assembly's annual missionary conference but concentrated on the daily patterns of life in Borneo and said very little about her own work. It was simply her personality. She wanted people to understand something of the place and the people to whom she had gone, keeping herself in the background. Even her closest friends (now elderly, but with good memories) say that she spoke little about her missionary activities.

It was during her first term that British North Borneo became Sabah, a state within the independent Malaysian federation and before long new regulations were put in place limiting missionary residency. Initially the rules were relaxed but then further changes came. Joyce was able to return there after her first furlough

(October 1965 to November the following year) but would never have a third term.

Along with colleagues Joyce was able to continue working in Sabah until missionaries were either expelled or refused return visas after furlough. The Aitkens were given two weeks to get up and go, with no leave to appeal. The Smiths received a letter describing them as "undesirable immigrants" and instructing them to be away within three weeks.

Whether Joyce was actually expelled or left in anticipation of it is not clear, but the July 1970 issue of *Echoes* announced her impending arrival back in Britain. Her route home seems to have been via Australia as Mr. & Mrs. Pucknell (now retired) wrote of looking forward to a visit from her there. By October, though, she was back in Workington and on the Monday of the assembly's annual missionary conference shared the Women's session platform with Mrs. Parrish of Argentina.

Korea, 1971-1991

What should she do now? Should she go somewhere else where she could use her Hakka Chinese? How she thought and prayed this through is not recorded, but she was about to embark on work in a completely different language zone. In March of 1971 the Gospel

Hall Elders' minute book reads as follows. "Miss J. Shackley: Our missionary sister asked if we could send out a letter to various assemblies setting out her plans for a return to the Mission Field, to a new sphere of service namely Korea, and giving our full support after hearing how the Lord appears to be leading, and asking prayers on her behalf."

In early July it was noted that "Our sister would be probably going to Korea in a few months and when a date was definitely known a farewell meeting to be arranged, with a word from a local brother and opportunity given to visitors to say a word or two of God-speed." It was also agreed that the secretary should write to Echoes of Service "notifying them that our sister has the full support of the Assembly".

Mr. John Anderson was invited to the October missionary conference to speak about Korea. He and his wife had lived in Japan for some years, serving the Lord alongside his business. In 1968 they had moved to Korea and taken up full-time ministry there. They agreed to come and Joyce was to share the Monday Women's session with Mrs. Anderson.

So late 1971 found Joyce in South Korea. At first she was in Seoul, the capital, and once again she had to start with language study as well as adapting to a very different culture.

Learning Korean was unlike her experience ten years earlier with Chinese. It was normal practice for missionaries in Seoul to take a language course at the university. Joyce persisted with this for a year, but found it too much, very fast paced, with constant testing. She felt that she would have a nervous breakdown if she continued, and there was no Bible study included. She therefore dropped out of the course and studied at an easier pace.

This was in the capital, but she soon felt that she should move away from the big city with its many churches and many missionaries. In 1974 she settled in Busan and served there for the next 17 years. The pattern of her work here was, she said, very different from anything she had done in Borneo. Having said that, there is little record of what it involved.

The assembly archive in Workington includes large numbers of Joyce's 35mm slides, but unfortunately there is no written narrative to explain their significance. One thing is very apparent, however; her closeness to many young women. It is clear that her work in Busan was about taking the gospel message to young Korean women and then nurturing them in the ways of God.

On retirement in 1991, approaching the age of 60, she moved back to the UK and lived in

Cardiff, interestingly at least for a time on "Corporation Road", the same name as her old Workington home many years before. For many years, especially after the death of her father, she had developed a close relationship with an assembly in Cardiff and the believers there were exceptionally kind to her.

Her closing years were, sadly, blighted by dementia. Driving north to visit friends she forgot where she was going and booked into a hotel, her friends bewildered at her non-arrival. Having been traced by the police she was blissfully unaware of having caused any confusion. This was her last trip to her native county. She passed away in South Wales but is buried at the Salterbeck Cemetery in Workington with her parents.

Note: After her first three or four years Joyce was only rarely mentioned in *Echoes of Service,* although the *Echoes Quarterly Review* in 1975 published a piece by her describing day to day life in Sabah and Korea. The *Echoes* papers in the Christian Brethren Archive at Manchester University Library do not include a Joyce Shackley folder. My researches are continuing and when the history of the Workington Gospel Hall is published (hopefully during 2023) it would be good to include a much expanded chapter including her years in South Korea.

Resources and Method

As implied already in the Introduction, to list all the sources of data that have contributed to the book would stretch my memory beyond breaking point as the project has already lasted around fifty years. I will do my utmost, however, not to miss any still living individuals who have helped with specific chapters.

Sources have been many and varied but given that this book is about missionaries who were associated with the Christian Brethren movement pride of place has to go the the magazine *Echoes of Service* (now *Mission Magazine*, and in its early years, *The Missionary Echo*). The many highly informative letters that used to be published in earlier years are historical goldmines containing far more than could be used in these pages.

My personal library contains long runs of *Echoes* magazine in the 20th century, plus the very valuable but sadly long defunct *Echoes Quarterly Review*; as well as many early copies of *Medical Missionary News*. However, much of what is written here has relied greatly on the digitised volumes of *Echoes* made available through the Christian Brethren Archive in the Library at the University of Manchester. Past archivists as well as the current Curator and search room staff have been consistently helpful.

Unfortunately the Covid pandemic years prevented any extensive use of the Manchester archive. By the time I was able to visit in person the writing of this book was already substantially complete. Most of the further information discovered there on a few of the missionaries has not been included. Almost entirely I have used it to check for inconsistencies with what I had already found by other means, for example correcting or refining dates. Further visits will, I am sure, unearth far more information and there will be much to add into later fully referenced papers along with the histories of their individual sending assemblies.

The ten volumes of *That the World May Know* series by Dr. Fredk. A. Tatford, and its predecessor *Turning the World Upside Down*, provided brief outlines of the ministry of most of the missionaries discussed, although this varied. That work's principal aim was to discuss the missionary outreach to various places rather than to write mini-biographies of the people, and in most cases little or nothing was said about their pre-missionary lives. An earlier world overview, in the late-1930s, was the small book, *Look on the Fields,* edited by James Stephens and I have drawn on my late-mother's copy of this in several places.

Mission activities in some of the countries or areas have had books written about them and I have drawn widely on such. For nineteenth century China it was useful to read the China Inland Mission magazine, *China's Millions*, alongside *Echoes of Service*. Also in a less secular age than our own it was not uncommon to find material reported in the local and regional press relating to missionaries leaving for foreign parts or back home telling their stories, and even extensive reports of missionary conferences.

With these sources it was not difficult (with one notable exception) to put together short summaries of the overseas mission work of the selected people. The greater challenge was to discover who they were and how they lived before their missionary calls, and what became of them in their retirement.

This meant delving into the many available public records and the National Newspaper Archive. These have included birth, marriage and death (BMD) indexes and certificates, probate indexes and documents, census returns, electoral registers, shipping passenger lists, professional records (especially for nursing), military records, obituaries in local newspapers, as well as assembly publications such as *The Believer's Magazine* and *The Witness*, to mention only the most frequently used.

Some of the data have been accessed online via Find-My-Past or Ancestry. Others have been obtained directly, such as from the government's General Register Office, and its Probate Search service, plus the National Archives and the Cumbria County Record Office, especially the Kendal archive. These are all in addition to my own database and files built over the past several decades and containing everything from snippets to lengthy papers.

Acknowledgements - Specific Chapters

Many others have helped with work on the more general histories of the assemblies from which these people went. Here I include only those whose assistance has related to individual chapters. BMD, Census records and *Echoes of Service* could be added for each one, and to most, Tatford's *That The World May Know*.

Foreword

Eric Fisk, The Cross Versus The Crescent,
  Pickering & Inglis, London 1971.

1 - Elizabeth Wilson

Dr & Mrs Howard Taylor, *Hudson Taylor &
the China Inland Mission*, 2 vols, CIM, 1918
"China's Millions"
Cumbria County Archive, Kendal

2 - George & Mary Ann Spooner

Dr. Christina Lawrence
Dr. Timothy Grass
Marcos Gago
Spurgeon's College Library

3 - James Wharton

David Beattie, *Brethren: The Story of a
  Great Recovery*
The Penrith Observer
The Coloured American

4 - The Brown Family of Whitehaven

E.B.Bromley, *Men Sent from God*
David Brady, Brethren Historical Review, 2017
Paul Hyland, *Indian Balm*, Harper Collins, 1994
James Stephen (ed.) *Look on the Fields*
Mr. Norman Walkinshaw

5 - Thomas Wales

The Witness, March 1940

6 - Amy Wharton

National Archives
The Birmingham Daily Post
1921 Nursing Register
The Penrith Observer
Christian Brethren Archive, Manchester

7 - John, Edith (& Grace) Rothery

The late Mr. Edmund Messenger

8 - Eric & Dorothy Fisk

National Archives
Eric Fisk, *The Cross Versus The Crescent*
The Penrith Observer
Christian Brethren Research Fellowship, 1970

9 - Joyce Shackley

Workington Gospel Hall archive
Mrs. Marjorie Young
Mrs. Elizabeth Stannard
Mrs. Betty Smith
Mrs. Blanche Aitken

Commending Assemblies

Several of these assemblies (and others) have commended other workers to the mission field in addition to those whose stories are briefly told in this book. This list refers only to people who are the subjects of chapters or are mentioned in them.

Barrow-in-Furness, Abbey Road.
    James Wharton

Bowness-on-Windermere
    Mary Ann Spooner

Carlisle
    Grace (Armstrong) Rothery
    * Thomas Blamire

Kendal
    Elizabeth Wilson
    Thomas, Hannah & Cissie Wales

Keswick
    * Harry Ratcliffe

Penrith
    Amy Wharton
    Dorothy (Smith) Fisk
    * James Wigstone

Shap
    Elizabeth Wilson
    George Spooner

Whitehaven, Sandhills Lane

John & Edith Rothery
Edith Brown
Mabel Brown
Mary (Brown) Bowden
* Dorothy (Ashbridge) Frears

Whitehaven, Woodhouse
* Tom Frears

Workington, Corporation Road
Joyce Shackley (Sabah and Korea)

Workington, Westfield
* Christina (Taylor) Ratcliffe

* Missionaries mentioned in the text but not the principal subjects of chapters.

The Brown sisters did not actually go out from Whitehaven but were all born there of a family in the early Whitehaven assembly.

Thomas Heelis of Appleby was never in the fellowship of a Cumbrian assembly. A seaman, he resigned from his ship in India, and joined the missionaries on the spot, but a Cumbrian missionary he most definitely was.

The Future

This book has developed gradually over several years, and at various points other Cumbrian missionaries were considered for inclusion. In the end it was not possible to complete the research on all that I would have liked to include. If there is ever a second edition, or a Part 2, then I would hope to be able write the stories of the following, some of whom are mentioned briefly in the present book.

Central Africa:
Ann Fulton (Keswick)
Wilson Beattie (Carlisle)
Noeline Stockdale (Carlisle)

India:
Thomas Heelis (born in Appleby)

Spain:
Thomas Blamire (Carlisle)
James Wigstone (Penrith)

Morocco:
Tom & Dorothy Frears (Whitehaven)
Harry & Christina Ratcliffe (Keswick & Westfield, Workington)

I am open to suggestions but make no promises as to when or whether this may be possible. My focus now is on completing the histories of the assemblies.